Other great motorcycle related books from Veloce –

Speedpro Series
Harley-Davidson Evolution Engines, How to Build & Power Tune (Hammill)
Motorcycle-engined Racing Car, How to Build (Pashley)

RAC handbooks
Caring for your bicycle – How to maintain & repair your bicycle (Henshaw)
How your motorcycle works – Your guide to the components & systems of modern motorcycles (Henshaw)
Caring for your scooter – How to maintain & service your 49cc to 125cc twist & go scooter (Fry)
Motorcycles – A first-time-buyer's guide (Henshaw)

Enthusiast's Restoration Manual Series
Classic Large Frame Vespa Scooters, How to Restore (Paxton)
Ducati Bevel Twins 1971 to 1986 (Falloon)
How to restore Honda Fours – YOUR step-by-step colour illustrated guide to complete restoration (Burns)
Yamaha FS1-E, How to Restore (Watts)

Essential Buyer's Guide Series
BSA 500 & 650 Twins (Henshaw)
BSA Bantam (Henshaw)
Ducati Bevel Twins (Falloon)
Ducati Desmodue Twins (Falloon)
Ducati Desmoquattro Twins - 851, 888, 916, 996, 998, ST4 1988 to 2004 (Falloon)
Harley-Davidson Big Twins (Henshaw)
Hinckley Triumph triples & fours 750, 900, 955, 1000, 1050, 1200 – 1991-2009 (Henshaw)
Honda CBR FireBlade (Henshaw)
Honda CBR600 Hurricane (Henshaw)
Honda SOHC Fours 1969-1984 (Henshaw)
Kawasaki Z1 & Z900 (Orritt)
Norton Commando (Henshaw)
Triumph Bonneville (Henshaw)
Triumph Herald & Vitesse (Davies)
Triumph Thunderbird, Trophy & Tiger (Henshaw)
Vespa Scooters – Classic 2-stroke models 1960-2008 (Paxton)

Those Were The Days ... Series
Alpine Trials & Rallies 1910-1973 (Pfundner)
American 'Independent' Automakers – AMC to Willys 1945 to 1960 (Mort)
American Station Wagons – The Golden Era 1950-1975 (Mort)
American Trucks of the 1950s (Mort)
American Trucks of the 1960s (Mort)
American Woodies 1928-1953 (Mort)
Anglo-American Cars from the 1930s to the 1970s (Mort)
Austerity Motoring (Bobbitt)
Austins, The last real (Peck)
Brighton National Speed Trials (Gardiner)
British and European Trucks of the 1970s (Peck)
British Drag Racing – The early years (Pettitt)
British Lorries of the 1950s (Bobbitt)
British Lorries of the 1960s (Bobbitt)
British Touring Car Racing (Collins)
British Police Cars (Walker)
British Woodies (Peck)
Café Racer Phenomenon, The (Walker)
Drag Bike Racing in Britain – From the mid '60s to the mid '80s (Lee)

Dune Buggy Phenomenon, The (Hale)
Dune Buggy Phenomenon Volume 2, The (Hale)
Endurance Racing at Silverstone in the 1970s & 1980s (Parker)
Hot Rod & Stock Car Racing in Britain in the 1980s (Neil)
Last Real Austins 1946-1959, The (Peck)
MG's Abingdon Factory (Moylan)
Motor Racing at Brands Hatch in the Seventies (Parker)
Motor Racing at Brands Hatch in the Eighties (Parker)
Motor Racing at Crystal Palace (Collins)
Motor Racing at Goodwood in the Sixties (Gardiner)
Motor Racing at Nassau in the 1950s & 1960s (O'Neil)
Motor Racing at Oulton Park in the 1960s (McFadyen)
Motor Racing at Oulton Park in the 1970s (McFadyen)
Motor Racing at Thruxton in the 1970s (Grant-Braham)
Motor Racing at Thruxton in the 1980s (Grant-Braham)
Superprix – The Story of Birmingham Motor Race (Page & Collins)
Three Wheelers (Bobbitt)

General
BMW Boxer Twins 1970-1995 Bible, The (Falloon)
BMW Café Racers (Cloesen)
BMW Custom Motorcycles – Choppers, Cruisers, Bobbers, Trikes & Quads (Cloesen)
Bonjour – Is this Italy? (Turner)
British 250cc Racing Motorcycles (Pereira)
British Custom Motorcycles (Cloesen)
BSA Bantam Bible, The (Henshaw)
Ducati 750 Bible, The (Falloon)
Ducati 750 SS 'round-case' 1974, The Book of the (Falloon)
Ducati 860, 900 and Mille Bible, The (Falloon)
Ducati Monster Bible, The (Falloon)
Fine Art of the Motorcycle Engine, The (Peirce)
France: the essential guide for car enthusiasts – 200 things for the car enthusiast to see and do (Parish)
Funky Mopeds (Skelton)
Italian Café Racers (Cloesen)
Italian Custom Motorcycles (Cloesen)
Japanese Customs (Cloesen)
Kawasaki Triples Bible, The (Walker)
Lambretta Bible, The (Davies)
Laverda Twins & Triples Bible 1968-1986 (Falloon)
Little book of trikes, the (Quellin)
Motorcycle Apprentice (Cakebread)
Motorcycle GP Racing in the 1960s (Pereira)
Motorcycle Road & Racing Chassis Designs (Noakes)
MV Agusta Fours, The book of the classic (Falloon)
Off-Road Giants! (Volume 1) – Heroes of 1960s Motorcycle Sport (Westlake)
Off-Road Giants! (Volume 2) – Heroes of 1960s Motorcycle Sport (Westlake)
Roads With a View – Wales' greatest views and how to find them by road (Corfield)
Scooters & Microcars, The A-Z of Popular (Dan)
Scooter Lifestyle (Grainger)
Triumph Bonneville Bible (59-83) (Henshaw)
Triumph Bonneville!, Save the – The inside story of the Meridewn Workers' Co-op (Rosamond)
Triumph Motorcycles & the Meriden Factory (Hancox)
Triumph Speed Twin & Thunderbird Bible (Woolridge)
Triumph Tiger Cub Bible (Estall)
Triumph Trophy Bible (Woolridge)
Velocette Motorcycles – MSS to Thruxton – New Third Edition (Burris)

www.veloce.co.uk

First published in June 2014 by Veloce Publishing Limited, Veloce House, Parkway Farm Business Park, Middle Farm Way, Poundbury, Dorchester DT1 3AR, England.
Fax 01305 268864 / e-mail info@veloce.co.uk / web www.veloce.co.uk or www.velocebooks.com.

ISBN: 978-1-845846-22-0 UPC: 6-36847-04622-4

For post-publication news, updates and amendments relating to this book please visit www.veloce.co.uk/books/V4622

FROM CRYSTAL PALACE TO RED SQUARE

A HAPLESS BIKER'S ROAD TO RUSSIA

VELOCE PUBLISHING
THE PUBLISHER OF FINE AUTOMOTIVE BOOKS

For Amy
"Have I ever told you,
how good it feels to hold you?"

And for Mom & Dad

Contents

Prologue

The Pole sauntered out of the café, the keys to his Harley jangling faintly against the chain which linked them to a thick leather belt working overtime. He stood next to his machine; it too seemed to have feasted well, growing fat on a diet of tasselled leather appendages and chrome hors d'oeuvres.

Casually, he threw a leg over his mount, his huge boot momentarily obscuring all but the horizon; then, with his bike still resting on its sidestand, he sank back into the saddle and turned his huge head in my direction. I felt the weight of scrutiny fall over me as his eyes flicked first over the Kawasaki and then myself.

"Where have you come from?" he asked, his accent a hard compromise between east and west, giving away nothing but the fact that he spoke better English than I did Polish.

"London," I replied. He looked uninterested. This irritated me unreasonably. I wanted this Polish giant to know, to fully understand, what it had taken for me to be sharing this car park with him and his gleaming 1600cc Road King.

"Originally," I said, and before I could stop myself, "But I've just ridden up from Moscow, before that St Petersburg, Finland and Norway." I quietly cursed myself. Was this what my journey had been reduced to, a pointless show of conceit? What was it to anyone else where I'd come from or where I was going? This was my path, my challenge; built on my own insecurities and home to my personal demons. Whether I was exorcising them, or merely exercising them was for me alone to determine, and while the motive for this madness remained unclear, I was sure it had nothing to do with impressing strangers.

Still, it did the trick. It was like hitting the starter button on his bike; his interest ignited like the throbbing pistons in that oversized engine.

"Moscow?" he repeated. "That's a fucking long way. You ride it all on that?" As he spoke his gaze returned to the Kawasaki, resting heavily on its sidestand a few yards in front of us. If the Pole had been searching Europe for a better contrast to that polished chrome behemoth on which he sat, he could have ridden for another thousand years and not found one.

The Ninja was camouflaged by a deep layer of dirt and grime. Its once green wheels were as black as the Michelins that adorned them. A rear indicator hung forlornly from its housing, the wires serving as a life-line, securing it precariously to the rest of the machine. The panniers drooped across its rump like great mounds of fat on a once lithe form. An exhausted bulb left only one headlight working, and its tired beam stared awkwardly into the distance through the remains of a thousand bugs that peppered the fairing.

It was a sorry sight. But, then again, so was I. If the Ninja looked tired and laboured, a worn-out packhorse wilting under the hot sun, its mud-splattered fairing and torn seat still exuded a quiet dignity; a defiance that hinted it wasn't quite ready to throw in the towel just yet. I, on the other hand, was beaten, and I doubt there was anything in my appearance or countenance to suggest otherwise. In the last couple of weeks I'd ridden 4500 miles. I was tired beyond belief. If any part of me wasn't aching it was only because it had gone numb many days ago.

I'd had enough, and it was depressing to think that after everything I'd been through, I couldn't find the strength to maintain a quiet dignity as regards my achievement. But the damage had been done, and from the dregs of my exhaustion leaked a little stream of hubris.

"That's right," I said. "I've ridden this Kawasaki up through Scandinavia, down through Russia, then back through Lithuania, Latvia ..."

"And how you find Poland?" interrupted the Pole with a grin. "These highways; shit huh?"

I wanted to tell him that compared to some of the roads I'd bounced across over the last few weeks, these were like finely polished marble, but I decided to play ball.

"I've had worse," I said. Then as an afterthought, "Have you ridden in London?"

"London!" he shouted. "The fucking roads in London are as bad as Africa."

I raised my eyebrows; it seemed a harsh slur on African infrastructure. I said as much and he burst out laughing.

"My friend," he said wiping tears from his eyes, "you make a fucking good point." Then he held out his hand in friendship and I shook it firmly, wondering whether this too would have him doubled up in mirth.

My Polish friend turned out to be a good fellow. We went back into the service station and, over coffee and cake, chatted a while about roads and motorbikes and where I'd ridden and why I'd gone to Moscow on this ill-advised and seemingly pointless quest. I had no answers – not satisfactory ones anyway – and the Pole, whose name I never learnt, seemed bemused, if appreciative, of my story. Later on, when we'd explored every topic that his limited English would allow, we returned to our bikes, pulled on our crash helmets and gloves and said our goodbyes.

"Have a safe trip my friend. It's been a long ride, huh? Where are you going now?"

"I don't know," I replied. "I'm not even sure where I am."

It wasn't a joke but the Pole took it as such – and a good one at that – his crash helmet only slightly muffling his laughter.

"I think it's time you end now, yes? Go home, my friend, go home."

He gave a quick wave, revved the engine, and eased the Harley back into the manic mid-afternoon traffic, his words lingering on the warm breeze.

Go home.

"Well, why not?" I thought. "That sounds like a fine idea."

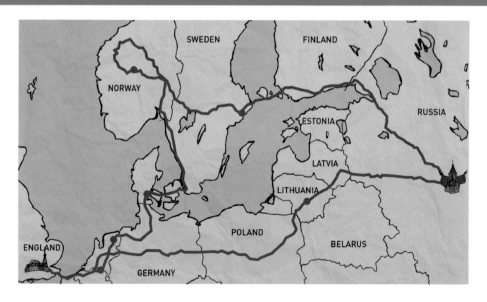

Three weeks, 6000 miles, and an ordeal in the finest sense of the word.

1
The beginning

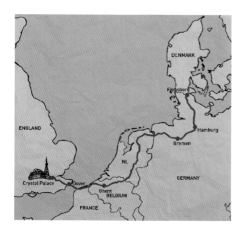

Crystal Palace, the start of a very special journey.

There's a need to roam that's hard-wired into some of us like a neon sign to a diner. It's hidden away in that part of the brain that howls in despair at offices and shopping centres, and it provides a direct connection between the thalamus, the right hand and the left ankle; certain doctors call it the suicide synapse. Sit still for too long amid the drudgery most of us face on a daily basis and the suicide synapse will snap, causing the right hand to roll involuntarily back and forth, and the left ankle to twitch up and down, usually following a simple pattern of one down, followed by five ups. When that happens the brain stem, responsible for governing involuntary actions, will trigger a deep preternatural response: some people just wander off into the sea, others swap their packed lunch for a shotgun; still others load up their panniers, pull down their visor and head off for a ride, and to hell with the details. There is no known cure for a broken suicide synapse.

Ghent

It was dark when I finally pulled up to the Blaarmeersen campsite in the pretty little Belgian city of Ghent, just over the French border. A slight drizzle hung in the air, the fine droplets of moisture illuminated by the Kawasaki's headlights, in the glare of which I erected my tent. I clambered inside and listened to the rain drumming a gentle tattoo on the canvas, a beer securely nestled amid my belongings. Outside, a little hedgehog scurried from the thick undergrowth and began sniffing at the tyres of my motorbike; I threw it some bread but it wasn't impressed, shuffling back into the darkness with a comical gait.

The rain drifted in on a chill breeze, so I zipped shut the tent and pulled my sleeping bag up around me, enjoying a peaceful contentment I'd not anticipated a few hours earlier. I'd spent the afternoon – and much of the evening – dashing from one wrong place to another, following good-willed, though woefully inaccurate directions, and questioning what on earth I was doing out here on the road again. For much of the last six hours I'd been either lost, confused or mistaken. It was exactly as I'd expected it to be.

The contentment I felt that night was welcome relief from the anxiety and worry that had built gradually over the previous few days, when the pressure of expectation, both of the journey ahead and of my own ability, had become quite crushing. Every goodbye seemed to ratchet up the angst a notch, each quiet moment of introspection led to more doubt.

And even now, with the journey begun, I wasn't quite sure why I was sitting in a tent on the way to Moscow and not at home in the warm, enjoying a glass of wine with my wife, Amy. It had something to do with age,

With the panniers full of angst, worry and excitement ...

I knew that; and the desire, the need even, to experience something other than work and home and the claustrophobia of London.

Life was catching up with me. I'd been running ahead of it for almost 40 years, but my pace was flagging and my knees were beginning to ache. Behind me, I could practically hear the rumble of a future I wasn't quite ready for closing in; the wailing of babies, the chinking of glasses over dinner party conversations; the rumbling groan of middle age, like an avalanche of years about to consume me. This was the inevitable future waiting for me just over the horizon; but if that's where I was heading, I would at least take the scenic route.

But the scenic route via where? Africa had all the appeal of golden cliché; I would visit that extraordinary continent one day, but not now. I wanted somewhere less obvious and, it has to be said, less challenging in terms of terrain. The pot-hole ridden thoroughfares of London were about as much as the Kawasaki and I could manage without risking long-term physical discomfort, so I needed some place where the streets, if not paved with gold, were at least paved.

Then, one evening, I saw a programme on TV about the waterfalls of Norway and a plan began to form. I'd ride up to Sweden, visit some friends, and then spend a while touring the fjords, lapping up that dramatic scenery and enjoying some of the fabled Norwegian hospitality.

"That sounds really dull," said Mike, a close friend who had an annoying habit of pointing out obvious flaws in the best laid plans. "You're going to write a book about that? It won't be very long will it? You could probably lift it from Wikipedia and save yourself the trouble."

I explained to him politely that he didn't know what he was talking about, and that he was, frankly, a bit of an idiot. But the more

... the adventure begins.

I thought about it, the more his simpleton words began to trouble me. It wasn't that he was right, not at all. Not in any way was that the case. But perhaps, through his ignorance, he'd inadvertently stumbled upon a valid point. Maybe a more challenging adventure was in order.

Russia became the destination of choice almost subconsciously. It ticked so many boxes that, after a while, it began to seem daft *not* to go there. It was exotic, exciting, a place teaming with fascinating history and contemporary thrill. And almost as importantly, I could incorporate a visit to Norway as a precursor to the main event. The idea cemented itself with so little effort that questioning it seemed absurd. I would ride up through Germany and into Scandinavia, spend a few days in Norway, then turn right, zip across Finland toward St Petersburg and push on toward Moscow, before returning via Poland, which I'd heard was also pretty impressive.

All I needed was time; so I requested a sabbatical from my employer, but after a couple of promising meetings and some noncommittal optimism, my initial request of two months was whittled down to a mere three weeks, for reasons I can't explain without resorting to expletive-ridden and potentially libellous language. Three weeks was a long time to sit on a beach or stare at a monitor, but to ride to Moscow and back ... via Norway? The whole premise suddenly seemed ambitious at best; at worst it was foolhardy and unrealistic. I'd need to ride as though my life depended on it, chasing my way through a dozen or so countries in 21 days in a two-wheeled frenzy of determined tourism.

"There's your book," said Mike. And for once, he was right.

So I found myself sitting in my little tent on the outskirts of Ghent at midnight, sipping a warm beer and reflecting on the day's ride from Crystal Palace. The rest of the adventure would unravel like a meandering ball of string, rolled first in the direction of Norway, then toward Moscow and the sepia walls of Red Square. That, in a nutshell, was the extent of my planning; enough I thought to determine a vague path of adventure and discovery, without impinging on that wonderful freedom that only a motorbike journey can allow.

Now the ball is in motion, determining its own path in a direction I hope will not lead to catastrophe. I have gathered up the first few strands and they have led me here, to this campsite, as good a place to rest and reflect as any. So I close my eyes and quickly fall into a sound slumber, and the warm fizzy beer slowly soaks its way into my sleeping bag.

I leave Ghent the next morning without seeing much of it, despite the assurances of the campsite staff that I am missing one of Europe's hidden gems. I am overcome with a keen desire to move and travel, to put some miles under my belt; if that means missing out on Ghent's treasures then so be it. Deep down I know this to be wrong; I am supposed to be exploring and enjoying, not rushing into the unknown with no thought for the present, but still, the excitement of the adventure is strong and I feel helpless to resist. I tell myself there will be time to re-visit Ghent; likely in a Peugeot with children in the back. For now, I want to fly through the familiarity of Belgium, the Netherlands and Germany, into the unknown delights of Scandinavia and beyond.

Flensburg

My stay in Flensburg in northern Germany was short, and resulted from the need to rest and re-fuel before pushing on to Malmö the next day, where I'd planned to visit some old friends. It had taken a solid day's ride, 11 hours to cover the 500 miles from Ghent,

A hidden jewel: Ghent, old ...

... and new.

What are the chances? I pull over on a random stretch of motorway, and what should I find?

up through the Netherlands and then, via Bremen and Hamburg, arriving at a little campsite on the edge of Germany in the early evening. It had been a relentless trek through heavy, roadwork-induced delays, compounded by a few very nasty accidents that had the traffic backed up for miles.

The ride was long and boring and, as the miles ticked by and the minutes turned into hours, I came to thinking again about why I was out here and what I was leaving behind. The home comforts and familiarities could fall by the wayside; I'm not especially interested in big TVs and central heating, nor in editing rubbish for idiots to sell to morons – the essential definition of my job. I gave little thought to the obvious risks and dangers of travelling alone by motorbike with only a puncture repair kit and some plasters should things go wrong. But already I was missing Amy. I couldn't shake from my mind the sight of my wife standing on the pavement outside our house, waving me

off and failing to hold back the tears as I rode away from her and into my own selfish adventure.

The previous night I'd opened my rucksack to find a letter waiting for me. It had been smuggled in there by my wife moments before I'd left and contained much love, some sadness and plenty of heart-rending sentences that I am too selfish to share*.

There would be plenty of difficulties to face over the coming weeks, many opportunities for regret and introspection, but nothing would prove harder than leaving Amy on that cloudy Friday afternoon.

Past Hamburg the traffic begins to thin a little and I start to look forward to a nice cold beer on the waterfront in Flensburg's pretty harbour. I ride past small German hamlets that are gone in the blink of an eye, and by the towering industrial chimneys that stand like sentinels on the outskirts of larger towns, exhaling an unending terminal

*That letter also contained instructions on how to order a cheese pizza in every country I passed through.

Strange goings on in Flensburg!

breath of rank black smoke. But as the sun dips lower on the horizon and dusk begins to encroach upon the day, I start to realise that Flensburg has an extraordinary ability to always be further away than it has any right to be. When it should be 150 miles away it is 250; when I am sure I have less than 100 miles to go the signs read '175 miles to Flensburg.' Upon reaching the place I'm amazed to discover I'm still half an hour away. It is maddening, especially after such a long day's ride. Eventually, I catch up with it just before Copenhagen and spear it with my tent poles to prevent it escaping further down the road.

I find a little campsite on the edge of the town and – after a horrible experience in the shower when, naked and covered in soap, I remember I need to buy a token from the reception desk to get the water to come out – I make my way into town and spend what is left of the evening in a quite pretty, quite relaxing place that isn't quite as pretty or relaxing as I've read it is.

Flensburg harbour, a nice place to relax ... for a bit.

2

Into Scandinavia

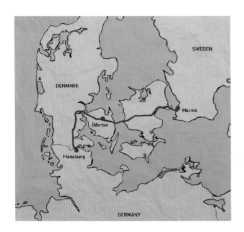

Planning the day's route over coffee and croissants.

Years ago I rode a Suzuki SV650S from London, down the M4 and into Wales. My friend Rob was on the back, enjoying his first taste of riding pillion. Rob is from 'up North,' which is London shorthand for the vast space above the M25 that constitutes the rest of England, where it rains perpetually on cloth-capped men in donkey jackets drinking ale in pubs with sad dogs and shotguns.

Like most clichés, there's a hint of truth to the stereotype. Rob is a tough northerner who doesn't take a great deal of shit before he stops talking and starts punching; he likes to tell of an annual half-day holiday in his village, when the shops shut early and the pubs are full by midday; it's known locally as Black-eye Friday.

But as we rode across the Severn Bridge in a force nine gale I swear I could hear him weeping on the back of that Suzuki. It was a horrible experience; we were completely at the mercy of the wind, which whipped us across lanes and into the path of faster moving traffic. Rob came back to London in the car.

If you've never ridden a motorcycle in a heavy crosswind, imagine riding a bicycle along a path lined on both sides with folk who really hate cyclists. At any moment any one of them may reach out and shove you this way or that. Now imagine you are travelling at 70mph and the people doing the shoving are invisible and are being paid on a 'per motorcycle crushed under a truck or car' basis – that's sort of what it's like.

I am reminded of that journey into Wales as I cross the first of four monster bridges on my way to Malmö and beyond. The Little Belt Bridge near Odense connects the mainland with the island of Funin, and runs for about 1700 metres, every centimetre of which I ride across in a state of absolute terror. A choppy wind and relentless rain have made for an unpleasant morning's ride, but my sour mood has been lifted somewhat by the sight of the huge white pillars which support the bridge and tower up into the overcast sky. It is an inspiring vision and I pull on to the hard shoulder to take a proper look.

For a moment I stop thinking about the wind and the back-ache and the distance I still have to go, fixating on the impressive structure and marvelling at its scale. I take a few photos, slap a Hapless Biker sticker onto a nearby signpost and return to the Kawasaki, and as the road rises up over the waters below I feel a wave of excitement engulf me, as one may feel when staring deep into the open jaws of a great white shark.

It doesn't take long for that excitement to be overwhelmed by a giddy mix of fear and dreadful panic. The signs before the bridge warned of cross-winds, but this isn't a cross-wind, it feels more like a highly concentrated hurricane.

The beating is brutal and terrifying. The drivers behind me must think I am drunk. It is impossible, literally impossible to ride in anything like a straight line and my deviations aren't slight. Before a hundred metres have past I've been blown completely across lanes at least four times and the cars and busses and trucks behind all have to brake heavily to avoid crushing me. I am helpless; completely at the mercy of this mean invisible foe.

I've ridden over some big bridges before, and the experience with Rob on the Severn into Wales was indeed ugly, but this is something else entirely. It's a strange feeling knowing you have practically no control over your immediate direction; that at any moment you may veer aggressively, but unintentionally, left or right with no idea

Another day, another border.

The first of four huge bridges, and the last time I would feel happy for quite a while.

which and no hope of preventing it. Car drivers couldn't possibly understand and I can't blame them for honking in anger as I veer across their path, missing their bonnets by inches. In desperation I slow to a snail's pace, dreading the crunch of a rear-end shunt, but equally fearful of speeding up, lest that vicious wind hurl me across the road into the central reservation.

There is a technique for riding a motorcycle in a cross-wind which involves relaxing, allowing the abdominal muscles, the deltoids and the forearms to flex easily and absorb the push and shove of the gusts, minimising the resultant movement in the handlebars and thus reducing the overall impact on the bike. I chose a different approach, becoming as stiff as a surfboard from head to toe, gritting my teeth so tightly that they actually squeaked and screaming a panic-induced fury into my crash helmet as I zigzagged onwards in a grimly determined and hopeless slalom.

It worked for me, but I wouldn't recommend it.

Almost by definition, if you have a Little Belt, somewhere or other there's going to be a big belt, or, in this case, a Great Belt. At nearly 7km in length, the Great Belt dwarfs its little brother, and that worried me considerably. Before I crossed the Great Belt bridge (or Storebæltsbroen) I pulled into a lay-by in the hope of finding God; I wanted help, or at least answers and maybe the chance to apologise; but He wasn't there, not that I could see anyway. Maybe if I'd looked harder I might have noticed traces of Him in that enormous construction that loomed in the distance, rising out of the white-flecked sea like the pale spine of a leviathan. There had to be something more than concrete and steel holding it up.

At that moment, the Storebæltsbroen became to me less a facilitator of movement and more a very powerful psychological

barrier, which brought my progress to a halt for several anxious and doubt-wracked minutes. The experience of crossing the Little Belt had been so horrible that I couldn't comprehend doing it again, not in those same awful conditions. But there was no choice, at least no realistic one; if I turned around and went home I'd still have to re-cross the Little Belt, and anyway, the option of giving up because of a bridge was patently absurd. It was, after all, designed for traffic; I wasn't crossing some Amazonian rope bridge. I just had to summon up the courage and get on with it. "Just cope" I told myself – keen advice that works in any circumstance, providing you're not looking for sympathy. So I rode slowly and awkwardly across the Great Belt bridge, and it was infinitely worse than I'd anticipated.

The wind lashed at me with a vengeance and the rain bounced off my visor like miniature artillery. The surface of the road glistened with moisture, in which dissolved any trace of confidence I had left in either myself or my vehicle. If I could have stopped and pushed the bike I would have done, but there were no options, no alternatives to this slow, inevitable progression. It felt like an unformed metaphor but I was too frightened to piece it together: something about life and destiny and maybe commitment, too? Who cares? I was in no mood for contemplation and, at that particular moment I had not the spare mental capacity to think, breathe and ride that damn motorcycle all at the same time. One of them had to give. So I junked the philosophy and soon after, the breathing too, and rode the last mile or so in a sort of stupefied coma, gulping down oxygen in short bursts when my starved lungs cried "Enough!"

When I finally rode off that bridge and came to a stop, I almost fell off the bike in relief. I felt as though my blood had been replaced with pure adrenalin. I managed to

The enormous Storebælt bridge. (Courtesy Sund & Bælt)

lift the visor on my crash helmet, and, as my trembling fingers struggled with the buckle, I couldn't help but laugh at the madness of it all. But as my heart rate slowed and the relief began to subside, a new sensation swept over me. I turned to stare at the massive bridge behind me, teeming with traffic like ants scurrying across a jungle branch, and began to feel rather stupid. It had been horrible, no doubt about that, but in truth all I'd done was ride over a big bridge in the wind. Inside my crash helmet my smile crumbled into a contemptuous sneer; how ridiculous to have wilted under such circumstances. "You idiot, Turner," I thought to myself. "How many bikes cross this bridge daily without a second thought, and here you are practically wetting yourself in fear. What a gutless wonder."

Apparently, an hour or so later the bridge was shut to motorcycle traffic; it had become too dangerous.

Malmö

After the Great Belt, the final bridge linking Denmark to Sweden – the Öresund – should have been unbearable, but was mainly just dreadful. I'm told the Öresund is very beautiful on a sunny day and I have no reason to doubt that. But there was no sun when I rode across it; just a chill wind flicking stinging rain at me and the prospect of a watery grave below. Still, the Öresund is a magnificent structure; its magnitude is such that one day people will use it as proof that aliens created us and the world we live in. It seems beyond human ability to even conceive of such a thing. Who in their right mind would look out over almost five miles of water and, with little boats chugging happily to and fro, going about their business in a perfectly acceptable manner, think, 'We need a bridge here'? But someone did, and one day I hope to meet them and punch them squarely in the face for making me ride across it.

In Malmö, I stayed with my old editor, who lives in a quiet little suburb with his wife and their two children. Dick and Cecilia Fredholm offer the sort of hospitality that should serve as an example to the hotel and restaurant industry. They are two of the finest people you could ever hope to meet, and I was lucky enough to chance across them when I stumbled into a job on a financial magazine down a little market street next to London's Waterloo Station.

We had a wonderful time working on that magazine. It seems in hindsight that every day something funny or interesting or potentially career-wrecking happened,

Dave O'Byrne runs the excellent motorcycle travel website (www.motorbikeeurope.com) from his office in Copenhagen. When I returned home, I asked Dave how he copes with crossing those huge bridges on an almost daily basis. This was his advice, and a better example of gallows humour I doubt you'll find: "Slow down, or speed up, depending on the situation ... just hope there are no cars nearby. If the road over the bridge is clear, I always take the middle lane, so there's room for a re-adjustment of trajectory, before you hit the barrier. If you do hit the barrier, and you do start to fly, and there's water below you, make sure you get your helmet off before you hit the water, as the impact might snap your neck if you land badly. If there's no water, I'd keep the helmet where it is."

Same day, different border!

and we took it all in our stride as we drank our way through the hospitality budgets of the world's banks. We made for a great team: Dick – my editor – understood the subject well but couldn't string a written sentence together if you paid him, which they did. So he got me to write his copy and, in exchange, he turned a blind eye to my abysmal punctuality and total lack of industry knowledge.

We muddled through like two chimps driving a train, and when the end of the line beckoned and the journey came to an abrupt end, more than one passenger asked for their money back. But it was all gone, along with the magazine and our prospects as respectable journalists on the FT. Dick fled back to Sweden, taking his soon-to-be bride with him, while I wrote a heavily fictionalised CV and tried to start again. But things were never the same after that job, everywhere was as dull and boring as

you might expect financial journalism to be. Eventually, and inevitably, I was sacked from my role as deputy editor, so I packed my bags and decided to take a motorcycle ride down to Rome ...

On the afternoon of my visit, and partly in celebration of our brief reunion, Dick and Cecilia held a crayfish party (much to the delight of the children). A crayfish party is something of a Swedish institution I am told, but as I don't eat fish I watched from the sidelines with a plate of cheese and pasta, as the children, Biss and Rikke, annihilated a mound of crayfish in what can only be described as a marine holocaust. In a matter of seconds every tiny finger was tipped with an expertly decapitated crayfish head, like 16 morbid thimbles that jiggled about excitedly before leaping to their final resting place in, or around, the kitchen bin.

Later on, after the children had gone to bed and we'd succeeded in achieving a

My Swedish mechanics get to work on the Ninja.

state best described as 'a little worse for wear,' Dick and I rode bicycles into Malmö to watch a band and savour the nightlife. My wardrobe was necessarily limited, and my only jacket was still soaking wet from the ride up through Denmark, so Dick – who is almost 7 feet tall – kindly lent me a coat to wear. Needless to say it was not a snug fit; I looked like Stretch Armstrong as I peddled drunkenly through Malmö's side streets on Cecilia's rickety old bike. As Dick weaved his way through pedestrians, apologising in between hiccups, I was reminded of old times, when this sort of stupidity came second nature to two young journalists trying to make their way toward a better future amid the dazzling craziness of London.

The next morning, as he made their packed lunches, Biss and Rikke seemed not to notice their father's headache; I suspect Cecilia did, though tea and sympathy were not on the breakfast menu. Our goodbyes were short and sincere – typically Scandinavian – and after sweeping the Kawasaki free of excited children, I closed my visor to begin the next leg of the journey, up toward Norway, where I felt the adventure would begin proper.

3
Norway

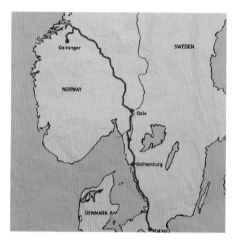

I'd been asleep for an hour or so when I was abruptly woken by one of the strangest noises I'd ever heard. It was about 11pm, very definitely night-time, yet not quite dark owing to the long hours of sunlight that make Scandinavian summers such a pleasure. So when I unzipped my tent and peered outside, the crowd of people gathered around my little home were clearly silhouetted against the pale blue twilight.

"What the fuck?" I muttered.

"Hello there," said a warm and kindly voice above me, "have you come to see them too?"

I stared in open-mouthed disbelief as my eyes adjusted to the semi-darkness: about 20 people were standing in front of me, most carrying binoculars and cameras with huge zoom lenses. I blinked several times but they didn't go away.

"See what?" I managed.

"The elk," came the reply.

"Have you seen them already?" said another voice in a hushed tone. "They are spectacular huh? Such beauty out here."

My mind, still foggy with sleep, was simply unable to comprehend this strange conversation, delivered in broken English in the middle of the night.

"What are you doing?" I whispered. "What do you want?"

"To see the elks!" Came the cheery reply. "We have come to see the elks."

"We're on an elk tour," said somebody else.

"It's a tour to see the elks," nodded another faceless silhouette excitedly.

Slowly, it dawned on me. "Elks" I thought. "This is about the elks."

Turns out, elk are a big deal in Norway. So much so that people drive out into the countryside in the middle of the night in the hope of seeing one, and I'd managed to set up camp in a prime viewing spot. As I slept, a small geriatric crowd had gathered around my tent, careful not to wake me as they tip-toed over guy ropes and readied themselves for a spot of nocturnal elk spotting.

But the elk failed to materialise, and so the group gave up trying not to wake me and

From the word go, Norway was wonderful: great roads and beautiful countryside.

began shrieking into the darkness, imitating elk cries in an effort to lure the beasts from the surrounding forest; and the call of the elk is not a soothing sound. Prior to that odd night, if you'd asked me to impersonate an elk, I'd probably have mooed like a cow, or maybe bleated like a sheep. I certainly wouldn't have made the sound which the man nearby was making, and of which I didn't think the human larynx capable.

I won't try and describe it because I wouldn't know where to begin, suffice to say that to my amazement and the crowd's delight, it worked. Two indeterminate shapes slowly emerged from the darkness of the woods and gradually moved toward our group, and under the pale moonlight they quickly became identifiable as an elk cow and her calf. They stopped about 30ft away,

calmly grazing on the long grass and their lazy contentment was deeply infectious. Our little congregation stood and stared in silent appreciation of those beautiful creatures, with only the gentle clicking of cameras and the hum of hidden insects intruding on the tranquillity.

It was a splendid moment, and the kind of slightly weird, wholly unexpected treat that made Norway such a pleasure to ride around. It's a magnificent, somewhat mischievous country, and like the trolls for which it's famous, Norway is full of wicked humour and not a little danger.

It was an opinion formed many hours before the elk encounter. I'd finally given up on the E6 motorway after another huge bridge had knocked away the last vestiges of my resolve. The wind was still gusting

The perfectly normal hobby of elk-spotting.

After this I decided I'd had enough, and took to the back roads, which proved an inspired decision.

strongly and the trees that lined the road were leaning heavily, as though prostrating themselves to some vengeful deity.

Wearily, I pushed on past Gothenburg, after which the traffic thinned a little, but the wind picked up again, and riding became such an arduous task that I finally gave in. "To hell with it," I thought. "This is supposed to be fun." I was riding so slowly along the motorway that I figured I could make almost as good time on the back roads up toward Oslo. The motorway was wide and exposed to the elements; off the beaten track, the villages and forests would provide more shelter, breaking up and deflecting the wind before it could gather itself for another underhand attack.

I pulled off the E6 near Hällevadsholm, stopping in a small business park to ask for directions. Here I got chatting to a very helpful chap who knew the area well. He

This is more like it!

told me the best roads to ride along, where I'd find the prettiest scenery and a host of fast flowing bends; but I couldn't help smile when he told me his company made wind-farm machinery. He was delighted with the unusually blustery conditions.

Once on the smaller back roads, I quickly realised that I should have ditched the motorway long ago. I had become too focussed on covering ground; eating up the miles at the expense of enjoying the journey. The route I'd set myself was indeed long, but far better to put in the hours and revel in that rare sense of freedom, the sheer joy of riding a motorcycle, than endure the motorway in an effort to speed up a journey I should have been savouring.

It was a valuable lesson, and one I would appreciate more with every twist and turn along the route 165 toward Halden. It was a beautiful journey; vast wheat fields lined the road for many miles, a vibrant yellow sea, interrupted now and again by huge lakes where the sun's reflection rested in a dazzling bed of fiery splendour. Along the shoreline, a scattered armada of tiny rowing boats bobbed about lazily, their wooden ribs old and fractured and their bellies full of water. The waves lapped against forested shores, dark and a little foreboding, where fleeting shadows hinted at wildlife disturbed momentarily by the buzz of the Kawasaki's four pistons, chattering eagerly in their cylinders.

For the first time since leaving London, I felt completely at ease. It seemed the journey had come to life the moment I'd ridden off the motorway and given it the space and opportunity to do so. I could begin to sense an understanding, a relationship emerging between myself and the adventure; one that demanded more respect than I had hitherto been showing and where my clumsy attempts to force an immediate destination wouldn't be tolerated, but which would

Off the beaten track, and Sweden suddenly mades a lot more sense.

reward me plentifully if I could only tame and contain my patience.

At Halden I stopped for a while, filled the Ninja's tank and realised I'd crossed the border when the attendant explained they didn't accept Swedish Krona in Norway. I took a walk up the hill to the mighty

Jo Cool contemplates the elk ...

Fredriksten fortress, a defensive installation built during the 17th century which proved particularly adept at keeping out invading Swedes.

It was early evening when I finally reached the Olberg campsite in Trøgstad, near the beautiful Lake Øyeren. Norway was proving itself a revelation; the scenery stunning, the roads perfect and the villages friendly and quaint. I hadn't worked out the exchange rate at that time so even the vast expense of all things had not dampened my enthusiasm for the place.

I set up my tent and went to find some food, returning 15 minutes later with a delicious pizza strapped to the back of the Ninja. I remembered fondly a time a few years before when I'd toured Normandy with my mate Bob and we'd done the same thing, collecting pizza from a nearby restaurant and taking it back to the tents to eat. That time I'd ridden pillion on Bob's Suzuki, clasping

Lesson learnt.

the precious cargo close to my chest to keep it safe. It didn't cross my mind that in so doing, I was holding the pizza vertically, so that when we finally opened the box all that remained was a sort of cheese and tomato sludge. We ate it, of course, but it was not what we'd hoped for.

This time I kept my pizza flat and the memory of that incident added a pleasing aftertaste of nostalgia to my meal. I retired to my sleeping bag, ready for a good night's sleep; little did I know that a group of elderly elk enthusiasts were already on the march.

Alesund, or not

As beautiful as the Norwegian inland was, my main reason for travelling to this idyllic place had been to experience first-hand the towering majesty of the fjords. But Norway is a big place and it has quite a lot of fjords; I knew there was no way I'd get to see all of them, but luckily I'd been talking to a chap from Bergen when I was in Flensburg and he told me that if I could only visit two sights in Norway, they should be Alesund and Geiranger. The south coast he said was very flat and full of beaches, while Bergen

We talked for a while, but then he had to bale ...

Lillehammer, with Olympic ski jump visible in the distance.

itself was always heaving with tourists. Travel a few hundred miles north he told me and you won't be disappointed.

I liked this old fellow, he'd ambled over to me with no encouragement and would have happily ambled back if I'd not welcomed his company. He was friendly and knowledgeable and clearly had no agenda; his curiosity had simply been piqued by this lone foreign biker and we chatted for a while over a couple of beers. In that time, he effectively wrote my Norwegian agenda, which was fine by me. The last thing I wanted to do was waste my time riding around aimlessly for days, missing the best of what the country had to offer. In planning for the trip, I'd spent about ten minutes Googling 'the Norwegian fjords' but everything I read said everywhere was equally stunning, which was nice to know but not especially helpful. In such situations, nothing beats the knowledge of a local, and it was reassuring to discover that despite the internet's apparent omnipotence, a good chat over a cold beer is still the most satisfying way to unearth valuable information.

From Trøgstad I headed north toward Lillehammer, where the huge Olympic ski jump is still clearly visible from the fringes of the enormous Mjøsa lake. From there, I pressed on toward the little town of Otta, every bend revealing yet more beauty, more lazy rivers, more secluded streams where youthful waters tumbled in excitement over weary rocks, like teenagers on their first trip to the city. I passed many campsites near Otta but I wanted to ride on, partly because the road was so inviting, but also because I hoped to spend a full day in Alesund and didn't want to ride too far the next morning. This turned out to be a mistake, because after Otta the campsites disappeared and the weather began to turn.

Eventually, I found a small farm where I was able to set up my tent and see out the last hour or so of daylight watching wispy strands of white cloud scamper across the sky, while behind them lurked bigger

It'll blow over by morning (it didn't).

Tears will just make you wetter: rain is part and parcel
of a trip like this, so no point moaning.

monsters, the charge of the heavy brigade with their blue/black armour and moist projectiles.

The night brought with it much rain, and the next morning I packed with little hope that the vast bank of cloud would dissipate. Alesund was still about 100 miles away, and what should have been a perfect ride through mountainous countryside was only ever going to be an arduous trek in such conditions. But it's difficult to trust your instincts when they so clearly contradict your desires. The cloud was coming in from the coast, in the same direction as Alesund; in hindsight I should have travelled south a little, toward Geiranger, away from the bad weather which was only going to deteriorate. But my guide in Flensburg had been so adamant that Alesund should not be missed that I pressed on, and with every mile I wished I hadn't.

By Andalsnes, with about 70 miles still to go, the rain had become so heavy that I couldn't see the road; a few miles later and I couldn't see the bike underneath me. Still I pushed on, skirting the shoreline of the Romsdalsfjord, but the great cliffs that should have been my reward were all but invisible through the dense fog. Roadworks added to the misery, turning the road surface into a slurry that coated my tyres and chain, and upset the Ninja's gearbox.

As the narrow road carried me from the shore of the fjord back up into the mountains, the conditions deteriorated further: the fog intensified, the temperature dropped, and the futility of the task finally began to dawn. It was simply too dangerous to carry on toward the coast; even if I got there, Alesund would likely be covered in thick cloud, obliterating the wonderful views and making the trip futile as well as reckless. "Turner, you may be hapless," I thought "but you are not stupid. Not this stupid, anyway." It was time to turn around.

My disappointment at not having made Alesund was tempered only slightly by my relief at riding away from, rather than into, the weather. I had tried and I had failed, but I was in one piece and that was a victory of sorts. With Alesund a lost cause, I pinned my hopes on Geiranger, a huge fjord about 70 miles away that I'd been told could pass for the eighth wonder of the world, providing you could see it. I rode back toward Andalsnes then took the 136 south, crossing a river and picking up route 63. Throughout, the rain continued to fall, a persistent and unwelcome companion, but as Andalsnes shrank in my mirrors so it began to ease, and the frustration brought on by the weather gave way to unbridled joy at a landscape that was never less than extraordinary.

A great, craggy, mountainous nirvana, where traffic was sparse and the silence, when it came, mesmerising. I stopped frequently to stare in awe at the harsh beauty that surrounded me. Snow-capped peaks tore at the dark clouds above, and white waterfalls decorated the rocky façades, smaller ones casually meandering through the mossy growth, while the largest plummeted to earth in a great raging torrent that seemed to capture the essence of time and timelessness.

I felt very small as I stood alone amid that enormous landscape, like a mayfly blown across an ocean; tiny and insignificant, just a fleeting speck of life, trivial and inconsequential in such an aged context.

One day, I thought, those great vertical rivers would stop flowing, but not in my lifetime, and which of us, if we're honest, can say anything beyond that matters? Our time here is brief, yet we feel a part of the unending cosmos, our consciousness refusing to accept that one day we simply will not be. I couldn't comprehend those waterfalls ever trickling to their sad, inevitable conclusion, just as I couldn't imagine the universe without me as a pivotal component of its great machinations.

No special effects; just the mind-blowing Norwegian scenery.

Such arrogance is hard-wired into the brain, but that doesn't make it right. Every river, each little stream and trickling tributary will one day fade to a puddle, before evaporating into the ether and becoming once again a part of that greater unknowable thing, above and below, without and within, where, for a time, " ... we float like a mote of dust in the morning sky."

Surrounded by mountains and waterfalls, I had never been so pleased to be anywhere, and at that moment I had no desire to be anywhere else. Should I even bother with Russia? Could there be any place in the world better than this? Then it struck me: "This is the work of the trolls," I thought. "They are playing mind games which I must resist, or else become a prisoner here forever, albeit a happy captive of this strange and wonderful land."

Norway, parts of it at least, does that to the mind, framing nature in a state of such profundity that it's all but impossible to walk away. "Damn you trolls," I said aloud. "You are cunning and devious, but I have many sights to see before this trip is done and I must push on." And push on I did, but my path took me deeper into their world, where fresh temptations lay around every corner.

The Troll's Road

At the top of the Trollstigen all is wet and white; the cloud hangs so low that visibility becomes a very relative term. But the gift shop is heaving, and the large restaurant is packed with soaked tourists: about a third are European, the rest either American or East Asian. The Chinese are busy taking photos of the photographs, unfussed by the horrible conditions outside. I sip at my coffee, wiping the condensation off my glasses and trying to ignore the dirty pool of water congregating under my table, trickling off my jacket in a guilty little waterfall.

I have not seen a troll yet, but I know they are here; you can sense them all

Mountains, waterfalls, tranquil lakes ...

... Norway has it all.

You'd never guess, but this is troll country.

around, despite the chattering ambiance of many foreign tongues. They are peering in through the thick steamy air of the eatery. This is their land and the road that has led me here is their road; how else could such a fantastical thing have come to be? The Trollstigen Pass, which translates as the troll ladder, is a twisted ribbon of Tarmac that snakes its way up this tremendous mountain in a mad loop of hairpin bends.

At the base of the Pass, a great foaming river runs alongside the road, its far bank consumed by the blackness of the woods beyond. But my eyes are not looking down, they are peering upwards: at the twisting, rain-soaked road and its impossible path; at the rickety little bridge high above that must be crossed if progress is to be maintained; at the savage rock face, drenched and bleak, it's scale hidden by the heavy cloud that rests a hundred feet above. This is troll country, no

doubt; a place of fairy tales and folklore, of beauty and triumph and sadness and, unless I'm very careful on this slippery road, a place of bruised limbs and snapped footpegs.

Motorcyclists are a lucky group; we experience things on the frontline, where there are no safety nets and few second chances, and if that sounds a little familiar, it's because its part and parcel of our world. The risks are high, but the rewards are many, and riding a motorcycle up the Trollstigen Pass is one of the finest rewards I have yet received.

Even as I slipped the clutch and heaved the Kawasaki around the next switchback, careful not to over-compensate for the heavy panniers compromising the rear suspension, I couldn't wipe the smile off my face. The path was precarious and narrow, requiring the use of both lanes to navigate the tight angles of the bends, difficult for

The Trollstigen Pass – a devilish piece of road.

smaller vehicles but a nightmare for the large tour buses that routinely blocked the road, shunting backward and forward, inching on, like whales trying to escape a maze. I squeezed past them, nodding to those drivers able or willing to allow me the slightest gap, balancing the Kawasaki on the rear brake and grimacing as the filthy chain ground itself over the front sprocket, reminding me of that horrible sensation of getting sand in your mouth.

The little bridge which had looked so precarious from below was actually made of solid brick, although by the time I reached it I was deep into the cloud base and its distinctive features were all but obscured. For a few minutes I was blind; unsure where the next bend would come from, or where the road ended and where the slippery grass and jagged rocks that marked the edge of the Tarmac began; unsure too of when the next tour bus would burst through the fog, it's blazing headlights straddling the lanes, forcing an immediate change of direction that was most unwelcome on that treacherous surface.

Riding up the Trollstigen on a clear dry day would be a wonderful experience, the views astounding, the scenery a joy. But the mischievous essence of the place can best be found hidden amid the rain and the fog and the cloud, when the mind begins to spot childhood terrors silhouetted in the mist, and the trolls' ladder pass seems a wholly appropriate name for this incredible place.

In the restaurant I finish my coffee and am about to leave when a bunch of bikers traipse in, sodden and laughing in something

Nearing the top of the Trollstigen, and keeping an eye out for fiendish faces under the bridge.

like hysteria. They take a table next to mine and we chat for a while about the journeys that have led us to this extraordinary destination. There are Swedes and Finns and Danes here, but I've yet to meet another Englishman, and I enjoy the status brought about by my unusual yellow number plate. Most of these folk are riding big adventure bikes, GS1200s and KTMs, and I take great pride in pointing to the bright green Kawasaki that stands out like a lantern in the dark amid the sensible machines each side of it.

I'm asked many times why I'm riding such a bike in this part of the world, and from a hundred possible answers, I settle on "Because it's mine," a response which solicits some confusion and a few raised eyebrows. It is not the ideal bike for these conditions

and I am not the ideal rider. That's part of the fun, or the challenge at least. But more than that, the Ninja and I are old friends; we've travelled many thousands of miles together and we know each other's foibles. When I throw a leg over the seat and turn the key, and the rev counter and speedo needles perform their little dance, it's like a lazy "Good morning" from a lifelong partner. And when I brake too heavily going into a bend, or fire the tacho into the red by catching first instead of second, I know the Ninja is rolling its eyes and smiling in exasperation.

But I don't have the inclination or the language to go into such detail, and anyway, I suspect every biker here feels the same. The story may differ, but the theme is identical; we experience the world with an intimacy

The first of many, surprisingly dull, ferry rides.

that windscreen wipers brush off and sun-roofs block out. We get wet, we get cold, we even get hurt, but we each glow inwardly at the prospect of 'the journey,' wherever it may lead.

Geiranger

At Valldal I had my first experience of a Norwegian ferry crossing and it proved a major disappointment. I think in the back of my mind I'd expected a skeletal ferry man wrapped in an old frayed cloak to emerge out of the mist, tugging on a rusty old chain to haul himself and his craft across the lake, but the reality was far less exciting. The ferry service was/is prompt, efficient and surprisingly cheap (about GBP5 per crossing, I think). I joined a queue of traffic and paid the conductor before boarding, then I rode up the ramp and squeezed in

among the cars and trucks and camper vans, joining a line of BMWs ridden by a group of chatty Finns. With the metal walls of the ferry obscuring the view below head height, it was quite difficult to determine our progress across the placid waters of the fjord, but the journey couldn't have taken more than 15 minutes because I'd barely finished explaining to my Finnish friends why I was riding the Kawasaki when the exit ramp clanged open and it was time to depart.

We exited in convoy and I followed the Finns for a while as the road took us higher into the mountains, until they stopped for fuel and I found myself alone again, riding up into the chilly saturating cloud and along the quiet flowing route that draped itself over and around the immense topography, like a strand of cotton on an unmade bed. After a few miles I noticed a small muddy

Breathtaking – my first sight of Geirangerfjord.

Cold, wet, and tired, but well worth it.

This stylish poncho, lent to me by my friend Bob, proved almost entirely useless and, once unwrapped, took up more space than a spare tyre.

car park, where I stopped to read an information sign; it basically said 'Look over there,' which I did, and then I almost collapsed with surprise. Ahead of me, like a scene from fiction, was Geirangerfjord; a massive rift in the mountainside, with colossal forested flanks stretching down into the opaque, motionless waters below.

For a moment I was breathless. For all of Norway's beauty, it was this almost mythical sight I'd been longing to see; the grail which I'd been so desperate to experience, but which I secretly feared I'd ride straight past in blissful ignorance. But there was no missing this. It was as extraordinary a vision as I could possibly have hoped for: the little village of Geiranger lay nestled on the far shore of the fjord, seemingly miles beneath me, hidden now and again by the cloud which swept across in vast sheets. But the cloud was beneath me now and so I saw Geirangerfjord as the birds might see it, a glistening treasure, glimpsed through a fractured canopy of nebulous grey.

The road down to Geiranger is as convoluted as the Trollstigen, but far more dangerous because you can hardly keep your eyes off the staggering beauty of the fjord. At another viewing place a few hundred metres further on I pulled into a minuscule car park, its contents overflowing onto the road and creating a jam as traffic tried to sidle past a badly parked bus. A carefully designed platform was built into the rock, and now, under the cloud base, the extraordinary view was unhindered; a narrow corridor of rock, hundreds of feet deep and pock-marked with dense scrub, casting dark reflections in the icy waters below, which escalated the drama and concealed the true scale of this mighty wonder. The full, irresistible force of nature seemed to reside between those cliffs, created many thousands of years ago by immense glaciers that tore asunder the landscape with a casual indifference, carving up the very Earth in their relentless progress. It was a privilege to behold.

To my right, the mighty Seven Sisters waterfall roared down the rock face, white torrents streaking the cliff, their power diluted by the distance, so they seemed almost delicate against the dark landscape beneath. Behind me, another waterfall tumbled onto the road opposite the car park, the splattering of water on Tarmac a constant reminder of the element which so defined this place. I remained at that platform for a long time, and, with hindsight, I wish I'd stayed to watch the sun set, although, by the time night fell, the rain was falling heavily and I was tucked up in my tent, surrounded by beer and improvised sandwiches and wishing I never had to leave.

Those damn trolls again.

We were hitting it off nicely until ...

... I found out she had kids.

4

Eastbound

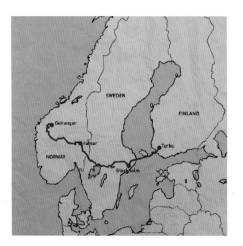

The road out of Geiranger was perhaps more impressive than the road in, although by definition it lacked that critical element of surprise which had made my arrival so unforgettable. The morning was clear and the sky above blue, but the sun had yet to warm the air, and, as I rode higher into the mountains, the chill began to take hold. I pulled into a rocky lay-by and draped my gloves, still soaking from the previous day, across the Kawasaki's exhaust to dry. There is little worse than clambering out of a cosy sleeping bag and into wet clothes: wet boots, wet crash helmet, wet leathers, and worst of all, wet gloves; like pulling on a fish.

But this is a minor gripe given the places I have seen and those I am yet to experience

on this magical journey. Soon the sun is climbing into its vast blue playground and I feel like my bones are drying out along with my clothes in the warm morning breeze. I ride past Innvik and Klakegg, following the twisting contours of the mountain roads toward Sogndal; hopping on and off ferries, stopping every few miles to take another picture of another astounding scene, chatting to fellow bikers doing the same thing. But they are heading up to the fjords, or maybe back home; none have their sights set on Moscow. I have a long way to go and a short time to get there, but after riding north for so long, I am now eastbound, heading into the sun with my shadow struggling to keep up.

There is a stave church not too far away that I'm keen to see, so I head toward Borgund, passing through huge tunnels that carve a neat path through the mountains; most are three or four kilometres long, but some are over seven. Inside, the bare rock walls are illuminated by a row of dim bulbs overhead, which are adequate but no more and I'm glad I'm not wearing a dark visor. The traffic is light but the big trucks are intimidating in such narrow confines, and at times I struggle to contain a claustrophobic panic. I don't enjoy the tunnels but I remind myself they are preferable to the bridges.

Borgund is a tiny village just off the E16; in fact, I'm not even sure it's a village, it

I watched this cloud drift all the way around the fjord, like a living thing.

Drying my gloves on the Ninja's exhaust.

Not a bad way to start the day.

There's one!

The Norwegian tunnels are often three or four kilometres long, and quite claustrophobic.

might just be a visitor centre, a graveyard and the creepiest little church you'll find this side of Amityville. There is nowhere I would least like to spend a night; but under pale blue mid-afternoon skies, this 10th century wooden building is exquisite. It's smaller than I'd expected, but so finely detailed that you could spend all day admiring the craftsmanship. It's a testament to whoever maintains it that I struggled to accept it was the genuine article, not some latter day recreation. It's in extraordinary condition for a wooden structure almost a thousand years old. Finely carved dragons' heads stare out from the roof, more sinister than any gargoyle, while the intricacy of the entire structure lends it a timeless fairy tale quality. Still, it is bloody spooky and I was glad that a handful of Chinese tourists were lingering around, laughing and joking as they photographed each other photographing the gravestones.

After Borgund I had intended to ride to Gol on the route 52, but at the last minute I changed my mind and carried on along the scenic E16, heading toward Lomen. This proved a bad mistake because, as it turned out, much of that part of the E16 has yet to be built. The Ninja is not at home on loose gravel, and my progress was slow as I weaved my way along the dusty surface, sure the road would appear again soon. But it didn't, and I found myself facing that awkward dilemma: do I continue in the hope that things improve, or turn around and waste an hour's daylight riding back the way I'd come? I choose the former but it took about six miles before the gravel abruptly returned to smooth blacktop and I could press on again.

That evening I camped at a lovely biker-friendly site called Bøflaten, which sits on the shores of the picturesque Vangsmjøse. As I made up my tent I thought how I'd

The Borgund stave church, almost 1000 years old and bloody creepy.

A wrong turn leads to a long and uncomfortable few hours.

never have found this lovely spot if I hadn't earlier struggled along that non-existent E16. A negative here, a positive there, things generally balance out at the end of the day and silver linings are never far away, you just have to look for them with the right kind of eyes. That said, such perspective is far easier to find amid the beauty of the Norwegian countryside than behind a desk in South London; still, I felt a lesson had been learnt, or at least registered.

It was at that campsite, too, where I realised many of my obsessions and petty fears around cleanliness were melting away. The ability to market hygiene must be one of the great success stories of our time; selling the fear of microscopic horrors hidden on every surface is big business, and I am not immune to this nonsense: I hate using public toilets, detest sitting on the filthy seats of London's buses; hotel bathrooms bring me out in a cold sweat. But now I found myself casually walking barefoot across the toilet cubicle, indifferent to the billions of bacteria keen to unleash their arsenal of germ

warfare. I felt quite liberated when I realised the shower held no dread beyond that of the water stopping mid-shampoo.

For the next few weeks I would shun deodorant and soap, and, wherever possible, use clean simple water to wash away the day's grime. I felt all the better for it, although I knew this newfound freedom would be over the minute I returned home. No one minds if you stink on a motorbike; some even expect it of you. But try explaining that fresh natural scent to a wife who won't come near you. "Enjoy it while you can, Turner" I sighed.

I spend the next couple of days gradually heading east, past Leira and Gjøvik, back through Hamar and onwards to Stockholm, where I will catch an overnight or early morning ferry to Finland. I had nothing booked because I wasn't quite sure when I'd arrive, but I figured they'd be able to accommodate a motorbike if I just turned up looking desperate. Failing that, I'd simply refuse to leave the terminal until they helped me; I looked and smelled like a tramp, and

A view like this puts things into perspective.

I wasn't averse to yelling at passers-by if I thought it might encourage the staff to squeeze me onto the next boat. But I'll deal with such issues if and when they arise; for now I am simply enjoying the ride.

As I sail through seemingly endless countryside, green and glowing under the late summer sun, I'm struck by an odd comparison that comes out of nowhere but which rings true nonetheless: the worst of Norway is like the very best of Wales. That's not an insult to Wales, which has some amazing scenery and is a very warm and friendly place to visit; it's just that Norway is so remarkably beautiful everywhere. Even the poorest mountains are the equal of the wonderful Brecon Beacons, the most humble lake a rival to the splendour of Vyrnwy and Bala. And the roads flow with an ease that makes motorcycling a joy.

Of course, the conservative speed limits force you to ride with care; a little enthusiasm can end in a serious fine, but the country is big and the roads generally quiet and there are times when I simply can't help myself. The joy of scything between forests and fields, on well maintained, empty mountain roads is impossible to resist. The Kawasaki is clearly enjoying itself too. Gone is the nasty grinding sound that plagued the gearbox on the west coast and with the almost new Michelin Road Pilot 3s gripping nicely in the warm sunshine, we sweep through what remains of Norway and plunge deep into Sweden, the miles consumed with such ease that I twice almost run out of petrol.

I spend a night near Karlstad and the next day arrive early at the ferry terminal in Stockholm, where I discover that the only remaining tickets to Helsinki are hideously, prohibitively expensive. The alternative is horrible: "You must wait 24 hours for the next boat," says the lady behind the ticket desk and my heart sinks; but before I can

Two very clean adventure bikes.

If you were looking for a reason to visit Norway, here you go ...

This is what it's all about.

These lazy sheep were utterly indifferent to my frantic beeping.

begin screaming at random strangers, she continues, "but there is a cabin on the evening ferry to Turku. It is a shorter crossing and only 90 euros."

This is fantastic news; I don't need to sail to Helsinki, Turku is fine and the fact that I must ride a little further through Finland is more than compensated for by the crossing being a couple of hours shorter. I'm so pleased that I fail to spot the reluctance in her voice, as though she is handing out a very mixed blessing.

"That's perfect," I say with palpable relief. "I'll take it please."

The cashier looks at me sympathetically. "It might be a bit noisy," she says.

'Noisy?' I think. 'Noise is fine; just get me on that damn boat.'

"No problem" I reply, and hand over my credit card.

And with that the warning goes unheeded; the red alert casually ignored. I return to the Kawasaki and unload my bags onto the floor of the car park. I have about five hours to kill and there's no point leaving the bike straining under all that weight. Then I grab a coffee and some crisps and sink down under the Ninja's shadow, avoiding the hot mid-morning sun as best I can while still in theft-preventing proximity to my belongings.

The port is a very strange place; it is ugly and surprisingly quiet much of the time, a giant slab of banality until another busload of tourists arrive and struggle awkwardly down the steps, tempers flaring as umbrellas and bags snag on more umbrellas and more bags. The whole place pulses like a diseased heart, pounding spasmodically to a queer, distorted beat. It reeks of diesel and sweat and the few people hanging around are surly and taciturn. Like me, they are bored and restless and keen to hurry along the hours until they can be on their way.

I sit reading for a while, gradually moving around the bike to remain in its shadow like a very strange sundial. Then, as I stand to stretch my legs, I'm confronted by a young Estonian woman, her blonde hair just long enough to reach the bottom of her dress, which grows shorter with every staggering step she takes toward me. She's probably in her late teens and is grinning a wicked smile, informed no doubt by the three quarters empty bottle of vodka she's clutching.

This is going to be ugly.

She totters about in front of me trying to determine which of my many blurred brothers to talk to. She settles on the one just to my right and directs a slurred volley of broken English over my shoulder. She wants to borrow my crash helmet. No chance; but instead of flatly refusing her, I ask her why she needs it.

'Idiot' I think to myself, the last thing I need here is a conversion. But now I have one, of sorts, and I can't walk away because everything I own is scattered on the floor in front of me and I don't want to spend the next hour washing sick off my panniers.

"I want to go for a ride on his bike," she drawls, pointing to the smirking rider of a GSXR staring at us from the other side of the car park.

"You will let me have your crash helmet? Just ten minutes; maybe twenty, a quick ride round the town."

This isn't going to happen, but she is insistent, chiding and insulting me one moment, using her cleavage and ludicrously short dress to try and win favour the next. Neither works, so she begins punching me playfully on the arm, but her punches are getting harder and it won't be long before the alcohol dissolves the humour and those limp fists are directed upwards toward my face.

I hate situations like this. The firmer I am with her the more frustrated she becomes and soon that anger and self-pity will spill

Holed up in Sweden.

out in an explosion of drunken hatred aimed squarely at me, and all the while I can see the biker opposite me grinning, enjoying the show. He thinks it's a joke, but if she becomes violent and I have to push her away, will he come swinging to her defence? I am a stranger in a strange land, walking a very thin line between slapstick absurdity and a car park brawl.

Finally, he walks over and it becomes clear that he doesn't know her either. He is, however, Estonian and able to calm her down a little, and she appreciates the attention, forgetting me in an instant and beginning to flirt with her knight in leather armour. They share a few words, she laughs loudly, and a minute or two later they wander off together. I don't care where; I'm in no mood to worry about her as I pack up my gear and load the Kawasaki. But before I can depart she comes lurching back across the Tarmac, clutching

a plastic workman's hat with a 'Bob the Builder' sticker on it. Where did she get that from? The bottle is still there, a permanent fixture in her right hand, as much a part of her as the hangover will be tomorrow, but now it contains little more than air.

The alcohol has diluted any remaining goodwill and now she is railing at me from across the car park: "Fuck you!" she screams and there is no doubt who her bile is intended for.

She holds up the hat: "I have crash helmet so fuck you and fuck your fucking helmet, too." The few passers-by begin to stare and I know what they are thinking. "What has that filthy biker done to this poor girl? How has he reduced her to that awful mess?"

Things are deteriorating and I am preparing to flee when a hand on my shoulder makes me turn in surprise and

Has she gone yet? Hot, tired, and horribly stressed at the Stockholm ferry port.

alarm. It's the Estonian biker. He smiles: "She thinks I'm going to let her ride with me wearing that," he says.

"Are you?" I reply, genuinely interested.

"You're fucking kidding," he laughs, "but she is happier now."

"Clearly," I answer.

He shakes my hand and pats me on the back. Then he shouts something in Estonian at her and she takes another swig from the empty bottle and laughs; they walk away together, his arm around her, partly to feel her tight young body, but mainly to hold her up.

Two and a half hours to go till I board.

Will she return? Who cares, I won't be here to find out. I ride the Ninja around the car park and stop in a quiet spot beside one of the enormous ferries dozing in the sunshine. I do the same, relaxing in its shadow and enjoying not having to worry about being anywhere. For the first time in ages I am not the master of my own destiny; I have no control over when the ferry leaves, or arrives for that matter. All I can do is take off my boots and socks and enjoy the freedom that this temporary dependence brings. I wonder at the irony of finding such tranquillity amid the stark concrete of the dockyard, rather than overlooking a fjord or at the side of a lake. 'There's no point searching for it,' I think, 'you just stumble across it and enjoy it when it comes.'

Finally, with the sun ebbing toward the horizon, I join a line of bikers at the head of the boarding queue and marvel at the precision of the dock workers, who flit across the loading bay in their weird mechanical contraptions, unloading the Galaxy Stockholm like clinical ants eviscerating the belly of some huge moribund beast. Eventually, we fire up the bikes and join the flow of trucks and coaches, headlights blazing as we trundle deep into the empty, cavernous stomach.

Inside is organised chaos; the lighting is harsh and the stench of diesel sickening. I squeeze the Ninja in between two other bikes and struggle in the heat to remove the luggage. Then I realise I can't possibly carry the heavy panniers along with my tank-bag, rucksack, helmet and tent through the impossibly narrow corridors, and I don't have time to trek back and forward; I have to decide what to leave unattended with the bike. The tent, ground mat and a single pannier are sacrificed and I hope the hold is secure as I struggle to manoeuvre myself through the awkward wall of trucks that line the path to the exit. I feel rushed, slightly panicked and horribly claustrophobic, but eventually I pass through a heavy metal door and emerge from the oppressive darkness into a dazzling stairwell, gleaming with lights and mirrors.

I am a sweating, exhausted mess amid the ostentatious finery of the lounge bar. I should find my cabin, take a shower and get some sleep, but instead I buy a beer. From the crowded deck, I watch Sweden slowly slip away into a glorious sunset. It is a fitting climax to this part of my journey, sad and uplifting in equal measure. I finish my drink and turn to leave; then I order another. This will be a long night.

Ivor

My heart sank as I squeezed through the narrow door into the tiny cabin that would be my home for the next few hours. If 'small' ever required a definition, this was it; it was miniscule in a way I thought only prison cells could be, and I was not alone. On one of the two bunks that comprised the majority of the room lay a large, overweight chap, sweating from the effort of breathing and completely indifferent to my presence. I dragged my belongings onto the spare bunk – which in more luxurious surroundings could have passed for skirting board – and

Preparing to board, with no idea of the madness inside.

nodded a greeting. Nothing. "Kevin" I said, pointing to my chest and refusing to accept his indifference as the culmination of our acquaintance. An essentially bald head rolled slightly to the right, forcing air from the nasal passages in a loud gust, like valves opening; the eyes tumbled in my direction with no obvious interference from the brain. I felt like I'd disturbed an ogre. He stared at me for at least 10 seconds before his mouth opened and two syllables plopped out: "I-vor."

"Hello, Ivor," I replied and he smiled wearily back at me, then turned away and closed his eyes. Was he being rude? I doubted it. In this tiny cabin there was simply no room for casual politeness. Any space not occupied with bags and boots was taken with fatigue and discomfort stacked to the roof. From his appearance and lack of possessions I guessed Ivor was probably a truck driver, probably Russian. He'd likely driven hundreds if not thousands of miles to get to this ferry, and in a few hours he'd be back on the road, without the thrill or excitement of an adventure to spur him on. Ivor wanted to sleep, not chat, and I wasn't going to interrupt him further.

Still, it was difficult to do much in such a tiny space without making some sort of ridiculously exaggerated noise, especially when motorcycle gear favours the lavish use of Velcro. I hadn't realised, until I tried with much discretion to undo my boots, just how loud and intrusive the parting of Velcro could be. The more I tried to deaden the sound with caution, the more drawn out and rasping was the noise. Eventually, and understandably, Ivor rose from his impossible slumber and without even looking at me – which was impressive given there wasn't really anywhere in that room

The sun sets on the first leg of the journey.

that didn't contain us – grabbed his wallet and walked out, farting his irritation back into the cabin as the door slammed shut.

I had a quick wash, changed out of my leathers and went to explore. Outside was Bedlam. Everywhere, East Europeans drank and laughed and occasionally screamed. Women drenched in mascara dragged infants through corridors, banging on cabin doors and shouting at men with shaving cream beards to hurry themselves. Children dressed like pop stars or prostitutes prowled the stairwells, laughing and chasing each other across dance floors where their older siblings, or maybe parents, thrust lascivious shapes through the strobe.

It was like Gatsby after the apocalypse. The whole scene was one of slightly desperate abandon, mobile phone chic for a generation free of communism but still struggling to fill the void. How do you play at capitalism when you don't know the rules and can't afford to roll the dice?

I spent what remained of the evening in an Irish theme bar, the only almost empty place on the ship, drinking expensive lager and chatting to the Swedish barmaid and a Bulgarian musician who played Johnny Cash and felt like an old friend. It was an enjoyable few hours, but soon it was getting late, or early, and the drink was skewing my perspective. How many long nights have seemed like a fine idea at the time? Too many, and none before had required a long ride through Finland the next day. So I said my goodbyes, paid off my tab and stumbled back through the madness toward my cabin.

I opened the door slowly and peered in. Ivor was asleep, which was extraordinary because we were about a foot above a nightclub. The music below was pounding with such intensity that my belongings were bouncing on the bed. What did the woman at the ferry terminal say? "Might be a bit noisy."

'Welcome to the cheap seats my friend.'

Ivor rolled over and I feared I'd woken him. That fear turned to something like terror when I realised he was naked. I doubted I could sleep now even if I weren't cocooned inside an amplifier. His bulging white torso was just visible in the half light of my phone and despite the warmth of the cabin, I decided to sleep in my clothes.

But Ivor was no threat; just another exhausted passenger on that floating jamboree. Some poor bugger trying to make a living, hauling rubbish across continents for consumers to consume and bin-men to collect. He'd probably done this journey a hundred times and knew exactly what to expect; trying to steal some shuteye amid the chaos of a night ferry, his fillings rattling to the hideous beat of the latest smash hit. He's past caring; the frustration long since deadened by tiredness and only 1500 miles to go before he can turn around and head home. But I am merely speculating, building a story from nothing but drunken clichés; for all I know he might be the ship's captain.

Ivor's alarm wakes me with a start but he is up and out the door before I can check my belt's still done up. I don't see him again. It's early, too early, 5am, but sunlight is flooding the room and I check that the wallet I keep hidden under my shirt like a holster is still there. Everything is fine except the time and I close my eyes and drift back to sleep. Moments later the door is flung open and a woman wearing overalls leans in; she shouts at me in a good-natured tone and leaves. I am very confused. There is plenty of activity going on outside, but why? We don't arrive for another hour.

Oh shit.

The time difference – there is an hour between Stockholm and Helsinki that I have not accounted for. It is almost 6.30am and for all I know we have already docked. I haul on my leathers and grab my belongings in a mad

Dawn in Turku, and a savage day awaits.

rush to get back to the car deck, where my pannier and tent are waiting to be stolen.

Overnight the ship's corridors have shrunk in width but grown tenfold in length; how can it possibly be this far? 'Because you're lost you fucking idiot,' I think to myself as I struggle up and down stairs in desperation. Finally, I see a row of bikes at the end of a scrum of buses, packed in so tight I have to squeeze through in a sideways motion. The buses are starting their engines and if one of them should move even slightly it will probably crush me. This is horrible.

By the time I reach my bike I am panting like a rabid dog and sweating booze. All the other riders sit waiting on their machines. Some are laughing at me, others look sceptical, as though the likelihood of me successfully riding this motorcycle as far as the exit ramp is very small. I don't yet know it, but this mad panicked scramble through endless queues of stationary trucks and buses will prove a most representative taster of what the next few days have in store. More than once I shall wish I'd stayed put on that boat and drifted back to Sweden. But as the jaws of the ferry open onto a crisp and clear Finnish morning, I know only that somewhere in the distance, Russia is waiting for me.

5

East meets West

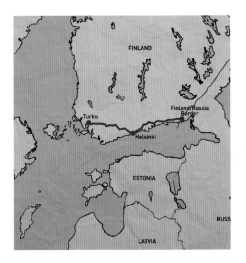

Turku is asleep as I ride through its quiet, empty backstreets. Another Saturday night has collapsed into the familiar wreckage of a Sunday morning, and I feel nervous and wired. Last night's alcohol is still coursing through my veins, and, coupled with the absence of food and the few hours' sleep I've had, I feel like an accident waiting to happen. And I am in Finland. 'Finland.' I repeat the word over in my head, trying to comprehend it. It seems impossible that I can be out here, so far away from home, on a sleepy Sunday morning all by myself.

The Ninja growls as we ride out of the docks and through the industrial heart of the city. At a crossing I notice a huge black swan wearing a golden crown staring down at me from the side of a building: an ominous portent or just a nice piece of graffiti? Either way, I'm too tense to stop for a photo. Instead I ride on, following signs toward the E18 and trying to get my head around this weird reality. I stop for fuel – petrol for the bike, coffee for myself – and slip on a thermal layer= underneath my jacket. With the warmth and the caffeine comes a new confidence, a touch of nervous excitement and the desire to push on. Soon I am tearing along the near empty E18, the Ninja howling in delight as we surge forward under the low morning sun.

The road remains mercilessly free of traffic until I near the capital, Helsinki. It emerges on the horizon like the last city in a dying world; a haven among the forest, where human beings can feel safe as the planet crumbles around them. On any other day it would be just another polluting metropolis, but Sunday mornings have this effect on me, particularly when I am riding my motorbike along empty roads in a foreign land. Right now, Helsinki could be on Mars and I the last Martian. Ah, but this is the hangover talking.

My knowledge of Helsinki is scant, informed solely by the music of '80s hair metal band Hanoi Rocks, whose ramshackle riffs and junkie-chic image practically defined my teenage years. As I ride past

Bringing a little Finnish glam to the West Midlands.

the city, those Friday nights spent back-combing my hair, riddled with teenage angst and cheap vodka, seem very far away. But the intro to *Boulevard of Broken Dreams* can roll back the years better than any photo album, and I smile as I recall how that damn band almost got me killed every time I left the house. Cowboy boots and blouses and eyeliner didn't go down well in the small town I grew up in, where the farming community and the local thugs never tired of smashing windows and breaking faces. Newport, Shropshire was not a good place to be a glam rocker.

Neither, I guess, was Helsinki, so Mike Monroe and his androgynous cronies fled to LA, from where Hanoi briefly put Finland on the musical map. Until then, the only cool thing about Helsinki was that it had 'hell' in its name, and even that wasn't strictly true. Hanoi changed that almost overnight; they were the most exciting thing to happen to rock music since the Sex Pistols, and they might even have made it big, but for an ill-advised shopping trip in Mötley Crüe singer, Vince Neil's, new sports car.

It's probably fair to say that no story which began "We were out drinking with Mötley Crüe" has ever ended well, and it certainly didn't for Hanoi's drummer, Razzle. When the two bands found themselves out of booze, he and Neil decided to take a ride to the store to stock up. On the way back, the drunken singer lost control of his car and ploughed the gleaming Pantera into a Volkswagen coming the other way.

Razzle was declared dead on arrival at hospital, while the driver of the other car was about as far from 'well' as it's possible to be while still breathing. Vince was shaken and bruised but otherwise fine. Hanoi limped on for a while with a new drummer but it was never the same; the spark had gone – the fans knew it and I suppose the band did too because they finally split in '85. But their legend lives on, for some of us anyway, and after Helsinki, I couldn't shake the chorus of *Back to Mystery City* from my head for days.

The border

Finland came and Finland went and I didn't see a great deal of it. It was a sad reality of this manic adventure, part sprint, part marathon, that I could only do so much with the time I had; something had to give, and unfortunately that something was Finland. So I carried on along the E18, on a monotonous journey that I can't remember a thing about. It's strange; when I think back to almost any other part of that trip, vivid images spring to mind of roads and bridges and streams and service stations. But when I recall the ride from Turku to the border, there is nothing, just a big mental blank; even my notes are limited to the road numbers and the fact that I stopped for a sandwich.

Scenery and incidents aside, the one thing I do remember is the quiver of excitement that passed through me the first time I saw a sign to 'St Petersburg.' That got to me; I really was going to Russia. But St Petersburg was 200km from the Finnish border and for some reason that fact had not registered. In my mind – which to be fair was still clouded with hangover and slightly numb from the day's ride – I still had that distance to cover in Finland before I reached the border; so it was a surprise when, about 100km sooner than expected, the traffic started to back up and I found myself queuing to enter the Russian Federation.

I joined a long line of cars and buses and began sorting through my paperwork: I divided my cash by currency and placed it into different wallets, hiding the majority of my roubles to avoid losing the lot when the Russians tried to scam me. I knew they would do so; I had been told by enough people along the way. I checked my Visa, my driving license, my insurance, my entry

Lesson number one: before you get in, you must get out.

voucher, my international driving permit and the bike documents (MoT, insurance, tax, V5); everything was there, filed orderly in my tank back.

Actually, not quite everything; I hadn't purchased a third-party insurance document which was apparently a prerequisite for entry, or exit, one or the other. I hadn't bought it because I didn't really know what it was and finding out seemed an unnecessary hassle because I'd read somewhere that you could purchase it from Finnish petrol stations near the border. I'd decided to ask someone just before Russia, but the border had sneaked up on me sooner than expected, leaving no time to do so.

I figured I had two options; I could turn around, ride back into Finland and find somewhere that could help me, or I could chance it and hope everything would be okay. 'Fuck it,' I thought, 'it's only the Russians.' I took off my boots and lay down on the grass verge; it was too hot to worry about paperwork.

An hour or so later I pulled up to the little hut where the border guard sat waiting impassively.

"Passport please." He spoke reasonable English and his formality seemed contrived, as though he was really a nice guy but had to play the part of a pitiless monster. I handed over my passport with a smile and then resumed a detailed inspection of my fingernails, concentrating awkwardly on anything that didn't involve absent documents.

"Who do you think will win the Grand Prix today?"

"What?" I replied. I was too startled to be polite.

"Kimi, huh? I think Räikkonen for the championship now, the Lotus is looking strong," said the fellow with my future in his hands.

For a while I just stared at him. What cruel strategy was this? These Russians were more devious than I'd anticipated. Should I just hand over my cash now? Give him everything and beg for mercy. 'No' I thought, 'let's at least make a sport of it.'

"Maybe," I replied. "It's a shame Petrov isn't racing."

Yeah, name check the only Russian driver; get him on side and remember this the next time someone tells me I watch too much Formula One.

The guard laughed.

"Tell that to the guys up the road."

"Will do," I replied enthusiastically, wondering what on earth he was talking about. Still, I didn't care; this chap was about as far removed from the impression I'd been given of the savage Russian border guards as you could get. I'd had more trouble entering France. I was so relieved by his conviviality that I decided to chance my luck and ask about my absent insurance document.

"Oh I don't know about that," he said with a frown, "You'd better ask the Russians when you get there." And that's when I realised: I wasn't entering Russia, I was leaving Finland.

I will remember that moment for a long time. I will remember the sickness that materialised in my stomach, the pang of sorrow which overcame me and which manifested itself in an audible and pitiful groan.

It had been far, far too easy. Foolishly, I had allowed myself to believe the unbelievable; you don't just ride into the former Soviet Union with a nod and a smile and hearty "Good day sir." In my haste to enter Russia I'd forgotten that I needed to leave Finland first. Now the worst was still ahead of me and my resolve had been sapped by this crushing disappointment. And I still didn't have that damn insurance.

In between Finland and Russia there are three 'phoney' border stations, small wooden sheds where guards check your passport for no discernible reason. This transitional zone is tense, quiet and empty, and the space creates a deep sense of unease. You are completely exposed as you traverse this no man's land, watched from a distance by many cameras and, I have no doubt, many marksmen as well. A lone biker on a bright green motorcycle must have made for a curious spectacle and I wondered whether curious spectacles made for itchy trigger fingers. Were they laughing at this oddball on their monitors, or preparing to react with lethal force if I made a suspicious gear change?

Probably the latter; the Russians didn't seem to laugh at much. Not those wearing uniform anyway. It was chaos at the border and nobody was smiling. Between the lines of cars and busses and vans there was barely room for all the people who'd left their vehicles to mill around aimlessly, dragging suitcases and dropping passports, stewing in resigned frustration under the blazing mid-afternoon sun. I parked the Kawasaki and removed my crash helmet. 'This is more like it,' I thought.

Asking for help in these circumstances was pointless, partly because I didn't speak a word of Russian, but mainly because in this chaotic free-for-all, I suspected pity would be quite thin on the ground. I decided to sit tight, stay out of people's way and let the madness play out until somebody officious noticed me and sent me in the right direction. As it happened, that didn't take long, and a chap with a gun, who looked like he didn't want to shoot me but would if he had to, ushered me toward a kiosk, where a lady gave me some forms to fill out and then left for the day. At least, I assume she did. I took the papers from her, filled out my name, but when I looked up to ask what the next question meant she was gone and never returned.

Which was a shame, because of all the people at the border, she had seemed the most willing to help me. She even grinned when I cut my arm on the metal edge of her booth, her mouth creasing into a smile as she decoded my crude capitalist language. She regained her composure quickly, resuming a stiff formality and bringing a stern finger to her lips, warning me to be quiet; but I didn't miss the discreet wink that revealed she was human after all.

For about 15 minutes I stood waiting for her, dripping with sweat, frustrated, but no longer afraid. This was an experience to be savoured, because I knew, absolutely, that I wouldn't be doing it again. When it became clear that my standing outside an empty shed wasn't going to facilitate my entry into Russia, I traipsed across to another station, pushed my way into the queue of people and handed my half completed form to a character far better suited to the stereotype. He glanced at the crumpled paper, looked annoyed and shouted "Documents" at me.

"Which documents?" I asked holding up a handful of paperwork.

He leant forward, as one might when addressing someone really stupid.

"Doc...u...ments," he repeated, slowly and with not a little menace. I handed him my passport but he pushed it back at me without opening it. I tried my driver's licence, but that was dismissed with an irritable shake of the head before it had even left my hand.

Next came my hotel voucher, which received equally short shrift, followed by my international driving permit; this was my favourite because it had an old fashioned feel to it and looked like it had been forged to aid my escape from Nazi-occupied Berlin, so when the guard practically threw it back at me I felt the hold on my temper give a little.

I held his glare for a second or two,

just long enough to realise I was fucked if I didn't produce something useful soon. My mind turned to that non-existent insurance form; was that what he wanted? It seemed a distinct possibility, but I had no way of knowing for sure and no intention of revealing its absence voluntarily.

The guard began to get annoyed; I was holding up the queue, creating difficulty and turning his refined chaos into a messy shambles. I understood his frustration; understood too that I was the sole cause of it, but I wasn't exactly having the time of my life either and I certainly wasn't going to let a loud clerk in a fancy hat bully me all afternoon. 'You want documents?' I thought. 'Fine, take the bloody documents.' I rummaged through my rucksack and smiling politely, dumped every bit of paperwork I had in a disorganised heap in front of him.

"Documents," I said.

For a moment it seemed the Cold War would resume. But surprisingly, my action seemed to provoke a begrudging respect from a man clearly bored with humility and reverence. To my amazement, and I think to that of the people behind me who had actually stepped back a little, he began examining the pile in front of him, wearily handing each wrong document back to me until he chanced across my V5 vehicle registration form. It was the one document I was sure I wouldn't need, and it turned out to be the single most important thing I had on me.

That one hurdle had taken about three quarters of an hour to overcome and it was just the start of a long afternoon spent incorrectly filling out forms and being shouted at. The detail was impossible: *was* I carrying indivisible goods weighing over 35 kilos? What *was* the value of my belongings in the currency of the state members of the Customs Union? It was utterly bewildering,

until at last I began to realise that it didn't really matter what was on the forms, as long as something was there to hide the white spaces. The Russians didn't care that I had 15 T-shirts and two pairs of jeans, or that I had written down 75 euros when I was actually carrying 84; if the boxes were ticked the paperwork could be processed, and if the paperwork could be processed it meant everything was okay. I felt like Winston Smith watching the war unfold from the high windows of the Ministry of Peace. Here was Stalin's legacy being played out right before my eyes; an astonishing mess of bureaucracy and officialdom that had no obvious purpose other than to perpetuate itself.

Through a process of elimination and luck I eventually managed to complete the paperwork, finally gaining those precious stamps that would free me from this dreadful purgatory and enable my journey to continue. I was pulling on my crash helmet with the Ninja ticking over next to me when another guard strolled over, wearing the relaxed demeanour of a man with too much authority. He asked to see my papers and began studying a form that had already been stamped twice. He considered it for a moment, then he stamped it again and handed it back to me.

"It's okay. You go. It's fine," he said.

I didn't tell him I was going anyway, but I was suddenly struck by the thought of what might have happened had I simply ridden off without that final stamp. Would my back protector have saved me from a high calibre bullet? I began to realise that in Russia there was no such thing as a simple mistake.

It was a valuable lesson; one that had cost me three and a half hours, immeasurable stress, a bloodied arm and a very tangled brain, but I was finally – and almost entirely legally – free to enter Russia. The missing insurance form was never mentioned.

Getting into Russia

For someone who's only ever travelled around mainland Europe, where you can often ride through three or four countries without having your passport checked, crossing into Russia was an ordeal. It was expensive, tiring, and stressful, but it was also an exciting challenge. The border represents a genuine divide between nations, cultures and societies, far more pronounced and tangible than anything I'd previously experienced. Getting into Russia is not a simple process, and driving your own vehicle makes it worse. The following might help a little.

You will need:

- **Passport and visa** – obvious and essential; gaining a visa isn't difficult, particularly if you pay someone else to do the hard work. I can recommend Visaworld 24 (www.visaworld24.org.uk) which did the graft so I didn't have to.
- **Invitation voucher** – this is a bit of paper from the place you are staying that says you are staying there. Why do you need it? Because you do, end of. It costs about GBP20 and most hotels or hostels should be able to email it to you. Technically, you should stay at the place that issued the voucher, but in truth, it's the voucher that's important, not the information on it. This means that you don't necessarily need to know where you will be staying each night, as long as you have a form that says you are staying somewhere; important for a trip like this.
- **Register at your accommodation** – this is important, but again I don't know why. Just do it within 24 hours of arrival at each place you stay.
- **Vehicle documents** – MoT, tax, insurance, log book and critically, your V5. Take the lot and don't get caught out.
- **Driving licence and International Driving Permit** – the permit is a legal necessity but I don't recall anyone ever checking mine. That said, I wouldn't risk travelling without one, especially as it only costs a fiver and you can get it from certain UK Post Offices.
- **Breakdown cover** – not many companies will cover you in Russia. I used a company called PJH, which provided a good level of cover for a reasonable price:
- www.pjhayman.com
- And there's also that extra insurance that I never had and never needed, but that didn't stop me worrying about it constantly. You can buy it at the border apparently, but given the language barrier and the pervading chaos, procuring it from a Finnish petrol station beforehand seems like a good idea. I should have done so; it would have given me peace of mind if nothing else.
- **Visit Horizons Unlimited** – useful advice from people who have been there and done that: www.horizonsunlimited.com
- **Spasibo** – Russian for 'thank you' (pronounced 'spar-see-bah,' I think). I'm convinced that saying 'thank you' in a foreign accent is the single best way to get people on side.

6
Russia

The refreshing chill of the refrigerator offered welcome relief from the stifling heat of the last few hours. I grabbed a Coke, it seemed appropriate. Two ladies eyed me suspiciously from behind the counter as I shuffled through the aisles of the ramshackle grocery store, which sat in dusty solitude a few hundred metres inside Russian territory. I stopped to inspect familiar items – chocolate bars, crisps, toiletries – that all seemed slightly wrong. It was the packaging of course; the Cyrillic script was completely indecipherable, but you don't need to be able to read to know what a Mars Bar is. In any other country it wouldn't have registered, but here the irony was stark and unavoidable. What was it Warhol said? "The

President drinks Coke, Liz Taylor drinks Coke, and you can drink Coke, too." There is no privilege too great, no class system too powerful to resist this great leveller. Coca Cola, icon of Western capitalism, had achieved that which Lenin never could.

I paid for the drink and was almost out of the door when I realised the transaction had been conducted in complete silence. One of the women had nodded at me as she handed back my change, the other had simply stared, her face a mixture of nervous fascination and fear. I didn't want to be feared, not by these two anyway. So I turned and thanked them, which they seemed to appreciate.

"Spasibo," replied the younger of the two.

"Pardon?" I replied.

"Spasibo," she repeated with a smile.

"Spasmo?" I said awkwardly.

They turned to each other and laughed.

"Spa-see-bah ... thank you," said the younger one again, grinning at my awkwardness but intent now on teaching me at least this single word.

Nothing breaks the ice like a clumsy attempt at dialect. We tossed those three syllables back and forth for the next few minutes until they were satisfied with my pronunciation. It was so nice to experience a relaxed atmosphere again. Those two women quickly helped dispel any preconceptions I might have had about the Russian people

My first taste of Russia.

and I left the store with something far more precious than a can of fizzy drink.

Outside, a constant stream of heavy trucks and battered cars roared past the store. I stood and watched for a while, sipping at the Coke and gradually appreciating just how different this was to anything I'd previously experienced. Was it psychological – the mere knowledge that I was actually in Russia skewing my perspective and adding drama to the smallest detail?

Partly, but in truth everything was different. Not fundamentally, but enough to dispel any lingering notion that I still had a safety net. 'This ain't Kansas, baby,' I thought to myself as another huge truck rumbled past, flanked by two speeding cars vying for the same tiny gap in the traffic. Horns blared. Vehicles swerved. I crossed myself and fired up the Kawasaki.

It seemed unimaginable at the time that the journey from the border to St Petersburg would not represent the very worst that Russia could throw at me. It was dreadful in a way I was completely unprepared for. The M10 is a road without embellishment; a patchwork mess of crumbling tarmac, potholes, trenches and gravel, its surface pounded into parody by the relentless motion of heavy traffic. At its edges, among the detritus, stood a ramshackle collection of sad looking people, selling trinkets and bits of fruit. A broken line of hopeless faces dotted along the highway, like desperate refugees that had stumbled from the trees, hoping 'the road' would bring salvation. But it didn't; not to them and not to me, nor anyone else stupid enough to try and ride a sports bike along its decomposing surface.

All around, drivers desperate to overtake

hurled their vehicles into the path of oncoming traffic, only to lurch back across lanes at the last possible moment, cutting up massive articulated trucks, causing their trailers to squirm horribly under braking. Twice I saw cars pull U-turns without hesitation, veering recklessly across four lanes of traffic as though in a video game.

If the women in the store had confounded my expectations, this frantic melee far exceeded them, and not in a good way. Nothing had prepared me for the total abandon with which these people approached the process of driving. No wonder there were so few motorbikes on the road; you'd be safer on roller skates, at least there'd be less to hit.

The journey got progressively worse the further I went. The traffic increased and the asphalt deteriorated; each mile seemed to drag on longer than the last. I have ridden in many bad conditions: through rush hour traffic in the dark on a rainy London evening; around the suicidal Périphérique ring road in Paris; down muddy tracks hardened by frost; across Rome, where deserving panel beaters go to spend a joyous eternity. The difference here was that no one seemed to care if they killed you. There was a terrifying indifference to the fate of everybody else on the road; a myopic fascination with the goal and to hell with anyone or thing that happened to be in the way.

And it never let up. By the time I reached the outskirts of St Petersburg I was far too drained to feel any sense of achievement. The day had been one long assault on the senses, from the moment I rode off the ferry to the point when I switched off the ignition, removed my crash helmet and collapsed into an uncomfortable plastic chair at a tatty service station. Now my mind was scrambled to the point of meltdown and the prospect of riding further into the maelstrom in the hope of finding shelter

was too much. I had nothing left. The sun was setting, it would be dark soon. I had no idea where I was, or where I needed to be. No idea where I might find help, and no strength left to go on alone. I was fucked. And then I met Alex.

Alex

There are a lot of people in Russia and not too many of them speak good English. The chances of stumbling across one that did, in a near empty service station on the outskirts of St Petersburg on a Sunday evening, were slim; the odds of that person also riding a motorcycle and having nothing better to do with their time than to phone around hotels, procure a room for a stranger, and then spend the next hour riding through monstrous traffic to ensure that stranger arrived at their hotel safely must be infinitesimal.

Call it fate, call it divine intervention, or call it luck; at the time I'd have taken any one of them. Alex was seated at the table opposite mine, casually toying with his iPhone and seemingly indifferent to the world at large. At best I hoped he might understand the word 'hotel' and point me in the general direction of one. But as soon as he learnt of my plight he went to such extraordinary lengths to help me that I immediately became suspicious. Enough people had warned me to be careful of the Russians, and while I assumed a degree of exaggeration, there seemed every reason to exercise caution: there is no smoke without fire, and to stretch the metaphor a little, Alex seemed like an inferno.

After he'd made four or five phone calls and located a hotel with an available room at the right price, he began to write down directions, but then he decided it would be easier if he led me there himself. This made me very uncomfortable; where would I end up? Were those phone calls actually to a villainous gang of Mafia, informing them that a naïve Brit was about to arrive at their warehouse in the middle of nowhere and to start digging his final resting place in the woods?

It seemed a distinct possibility, but how could I refuse? I was hopelessly lost on the edge of a massive city, with no idea what to do or where to go; I couldn't even read the signposts. If I didn't follow him, chances were I'd be crushed under a truck as I tried to navigate the city alone at night. As Alex talked, I weighed up the odds: shallow grave or road kill? I figured a bullet in the back of the head would be quicker, so I shook his hand, pulled on my lid, and followed him into the fray.

For the next hour the needle on my speedometer only dropped below 70mph when we stopped at traffic lights. Alex rode flat out and with total confidence at all times, threading his Suzuki through the traffic with imperious style and seemingly oblivious to the massive risks he was taking and which, by necessity, I was forced to share.

I didn't enjoy that journey but I did learn a lot about riding a motorcycle in Russia. In England we are taught to position our motorcycles in the middle of whichever lane we might be in, so that we are highly visible, leaving no space for an impatient driver to try and force a reckless overtake. It works on the principle that no one road user would intentionally try to kill another. But that moral imperative does not hold true in the East, where dominating a lane will only result in you being hit from behind and left for dead.

In Russia, you must either overtake or get out of the way; there is no middle ground; no place for the pious driver who seeks only a safe and pleasant trip. Alex understood this and used the full power of his 500cc machine

Alex – spasibo!

My hotel in St Petersburg; a fine example of communist architecture.

to his advantage, maintaining a speed that meant he didn't need to worry about being overtaken and relying on his own instincts and reactions to dart between the vehicles in front. The strategy obviously worked because Alex was still alive. But it relied on such deft reflexes and such intense concentration that I struggled to keep up. It felt like an unending trackday, but without the luxury of gravel traps or medics. Eventually I began to fall back, finally losing sight of my guide as he disappeared into a space approximately half an inch larger than his motorbike.

I am used to heavy traffic and I am not afraid to filter; but when the closing speed is upwards of 50mph and the slightest divergence or erratic lane change from the car in front will result in my occupying its back seat, I enjoy it less. Alex left absolutely no margin for error, which I admired but was not about to replicate, certainly not with every single overtake.

I found him waiting for me at the side of the road. I felt embarrassed, as though I'd let the side down. But he just nodded and rode off again, at a pace I was able to live with.

When we finally pulled into the car park of the hotel, any concerns about Alex's intentions had been well and truly dispelled. He was insane, of that I had no doubt, but he wasn't actively intent on harming me. He was, and I'm sure still is, just a really nice bloke who went to extraordinary lengths to help a rather desperate individual. He even offered to carry my panniers for me! I didn't feel guilty about mistrusting him;

St Isaac's Cathedral; a fine example of pre-communist architecture.

his kind of generosity isn't commonplace and a little cynicism is no bad thing when you're travelling on your own. The pity was that I couldn't do more to thank him. Alex, if you should ever read this, Spasibo, you quite possibly saved my life, although it didn't feel like it at the time.

St Petersburg
Inside the Hotel Olgino, a big concrete monstrosity that could only have been built under Soviet rule, I was finally able to relax. I showered – what a joy! – and drank beer (also a pleasant experience), and then slept well in a proper bed and dreamt of being at home with Amy.

When I awoke, it was to a bright, sunny morning. Refreshed and revitalised, I made my way into the city via bus, joining the throng of commuters for whom the day would be like any other, with no prospect of surprise or thrill. But I was deep in the heart of an adventure and the grey tower blocks, the graffiti and the ugly over-ground heating pipes served only to heighten my excitement.

The bus lurched to a stop next to the underground station. Outside, the scene was familiar but the context so strange that I struggled to comprehend it. People were going about their morning as people do everywhere; but these weren't my people.

The impressive dome of St Isaac's Cathedral.

Not a big fan of heights, but the view from St Isaac's was very impressive.

Not Londoners, not English, not even Westerners: these were Russians. I was quite suddenly overwhelmed by the realisation that I was actually in St Petersburg. I was standing in Russia.

On the road I'd not given the subject much thought. I was living hand-to-mouth, hour-by-hour, day-by-day, and had barely had time to register the miles, let alone consider the wider implications of where I was going. But as I stepped down from that bus and looked around me, it was as though the whole trip suddenly came into focus. I had ridden to Russia: I wasn't riding there, or planning to ride there, I was actually there, and so far from home that the distance was all but irrelevant. At once I felt proud, afraid and profoundly alone. Although, strangely, not lonely.

I made my way into the underground station, and that sense of isolation was immediately reinforced by my absolute inability to communicate with anyone or

understand anything at all. I tried to buy a ticket but I was shouted at and shooed away like a stray cat sniffing at rubbish.

I milled about for a while, observing others and trying to understand what I'd done wrong, but nothing seemed obvious so I tried again, and this time the transaction went smoothly. "Spasibo," I muttered as I struggled through the rush hour queues and tried to match the weird symbols on the platforms with those in my guide book.

Somehow I did get the correct train, and when I got off at my intended station I was very pleased with myself; even more so when I turned a corner and the huge golden dome of St Isaac's Cathedral stood against the cloudless blue sky.

As the journey had progressed and the days slipped by, I'd begun to wonder whether I should bypass St Petersburg altogether and push on to Moscow, which had always been the ultimate objective. I was concerned about the time I had left and the distance

The Venice of the North.

I had yet to travel, and for a while, Russia's second largest city began to seem like a costly indulgence.

It was that slightly panicked mind-set revealing itself again; that part of the brain that kept telling me to get this whole caper over and done with as quickly and painlessly as possible. The temptations of home were not easy to dismiss, but neither was the fear of regret. What kind of an idiot would ride all this way and then rush past one of the world's great cities so they could return to normality that bit sooner? 'Not this kind,' I told myself.

No, I would just have to ride harder and longer, which was part of the fun anyway. It was the right decision. With its remarkable history and stunning architecture, St Petersburg was an absolute revelation. The people were friendly, the streets clean and litter free and the sights plentiful, but not too many to take in over a couple of leisurely days.

I climbed the stone spiral staircase of St Isaac's and admired the city from on high, then I strolled down Nevsky Prospect, peering through shop windows at the expensive luxury goods which must have been unimaginable to the city's populous a few decades earlier. Further down the affluent avenue I turned left onto Konyushnaya ploshchad – a long street running alongside a pretty canal, on the bank of which stands the stunning Church of the Resurrection of Christ 'On Spilled Blood.'

From a distance the church is marvellous, but as you get closer the painstaking detail of the building reveals itself with ever greater clarity. Both inside and out, the beauty was extraordinary and I found myself staring at the smallest sections of finely decorated wall and ceiling for a very long time, trying to imagine just how much effort must have gone into perfecting that tiny space. After a while of doing this I felt my brain beginning to ache, so I took leave and found respite

The extraordinary exterior of the Church of the Resurrection of Christ 'On Spilled Blood.'

Inside it's all mosaics; nothing is painted!

Imagine the size of the toenail clippings ...

From Crystal Palace to the Winter Palace.

Overcompensating? The enormous spire of the Peter and Paul Cathedral.

Like stepping back in time (if you can ignore the mobile phone).

The beautiful Palace Square, St Petersburg.

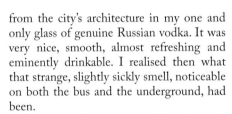

The Russian Starbucks logo ...

... looked a tad familiar.

from the city's architecture in my one and only glass of genuine Russian vodka. It was very nice, smooth, almost refreshing and eminently drinkable. I realised then what that strange, slightly sickly smell, noticeable on both the bus and the underground, had been.

I continued my tour, walking through parks full of fascinating statues and over the Dvortsovy Most Bridge, to stand in awe of the enormous glistening spire of the Peter and Paul Cathedral. I took shelter from the sun in the shadows of the quiet side streets, which criss-cross the many canals that give the city is unofficial title of the Venice of the North (although I believe Birmingham has more canals than Venice, so perhaps they should factor that into the city's name – St Petersburg: the Birmingham of the East).

As I made my way back across the Troitsky Most, which spans the enormous river Neva, I had my first sight of the Winter Palace, a quite extraordinarily beautiful building that was for many centuries the home of the Russian monarchy.

That Palace has witnessed the sort of history that brings me out in goose-bumps. The slaughter of Russian peasants happened here in 1905, in what came to be known as the Bloody Sunday massacre, when the city's workers marched on the Palace believing, mistakenly as it happens, that the Tsar was in residence. The army opened fire, killing almost 100 innocent protestors in a moment of madness that had a profound effect on Russian sentiment toward their leader and which led almost directly to the Revolution of 1917. During that period, the Palace was ransacked by the Bolsheviks, but with around 1500 rooms to ravage, the destruction took time; thankfully for those doing the ransacking, the Palace's vast wine cellars were available to fuel the mayhem, which lasted for weeks and which resulted

Wishing I'd packed the sat nav.

in what has been described as the 'biggest hangover in history.'

During the siege of Leningrad, the Winter Palace became a symbol of resistance against the Germans, and though badly damaged, it has since been restored to something like its true majesty. Even the Romanov emblems, so hated by the Communists, have been reinstated so that to the casual tourist, the Winter Palace now stands as it once did: as a sublime tribute to privilege, wealth and almost divine power.

It seems extraordinary now to realise the very clear lineage that began with those first shots fired by over-zealous soldiers on a ragged crowd in 1905 and which culminated in David Hasselhoff standing on the Berlin Wall in 1989, and which in the process takes in practically every key event of the 20th century, from the siege of Leningrad to the Cuban Missile Crisis and the depths of the Cold War. But it's all there to see with the right kind of eyes, although there's little of that communist history on show in Palace Square. Russia it seemed to me, would rather celebrate the exuberance of its dynastic heritage than dwell too much on the stoic breadlines of its communist years. And who can blame it? There's only so much dignity in the hollowed faces and clenched fists of the emaciated proletariat, and most of us would sacrifice a good chunk of that for a nice meal and a glass of wine, and to hell with the politics.

Deeper

Clearing St Petersburg was horrible. I was lost for hours, despite making detailed notes before leaving the hotel. But the Cyrillic script on the signs made it all but impossible to identify which road I was on without stopping and asking passers-by. It was such a long-winded and tiresome approach to navigation and I cursed myself for not packing a sat-nav. It seemed to run against the essence of the journey when I was sat at home and everything looked so easy on the map. But now, utterly lost in another foreign city, I rued my stupidity and vowed never again to leave the house without technological support. Eventually, a very helpful man who was sitting in his car and who may have been a getaway driver drew me a rough map, and a few hours later I picked up signs to Moscow.

Ahead of me lay 450 miles of ugly Russian highway, ridden with pot-holes, flanked by deep forests and occupied, almost exclusively, by an unending convoy of huge filthy trucks which thundered along under a thick cloud of acrid black diesel fumes.

Four hundred miles at an average speed of 75mph doesn't sound so bad; it certainly didn't the night before when I'd planned the run in my head and decided to tackle it in four stints of 100 miles each. 'A hundred miles is nothing,' I'd told myself. 'I do it for fun on a Sunday morning. Two stints before lunch and two after and you'll be in Moscow by six o'clock, no probs.' Which would have been true, if I hadn't spent half the morning trapped in St Petersburg and the rest of it practically in tears by the roadside, wondering whether I shouldn't just turn around and go home.

The M10 is a very long road, but it's not very wide. For much of its duration it is essentially just two lanes, one going north and one going south. This hampers overtaking, especially for truck drivers who must factor in the best part of half a mile of clear road if they are to power their massive machines past other, equally massive machines and not crash headlong into someone doing the same thing in the opposite direction.

To solve this problem, the designers of the M10 built in overtaking areas, widening one lane (slightly) and dividing it in two, enabling vehicles to pass one another without having to cross the central divide.

Yes, it's staged, but it captures perfectly my state of mind as I rode from St Petersburg to Moscow.

This happens alternately, so that for a mile or so traffic heading toward St Petersburg can overtake, and then a few miles later, traffic on route to Moscow can do the same. This would work well, were it not for the sporadic nature of the overtaking lanes. Because they are limited to every few miles and are quite short, there is a mad scramble to do as much passing as possible before the two lanes merge back into one. This inevitably results in drivers cutting up traffic as they attempt one last desperate overtake before forcing their way back onto their own side of the road, or more often as not, forcing traffic on the other side of the road into quite drastic avoidance measures. It is not an effective solution to

the problem of overtaking; far from it. It practically encourages disaster.

It is almost impossible to over emphasise the near suicidal danger implicit in riding a motorcycle along that road. If you relax for one moment, you will die. If you blink it must be a conscious decision, timed to avoid calamity. Take a moment to check your mirrors and you will either hit a pot hole so deep that it shatters your spine or drive straight into a vehicle heading toward you on the wrong side of the road. There is no respite, no moment to breathe deeply and reflect on how close that last near miss was because the next one is already happening. It is one long, relentless attack on the senses; a savage assault on that part of the brain charged with keeping you alive.

I found myself taking risks I would never have dreamt of taking back home, or anywhere else for that matter. But I knew that unless I overtook the stinking, lumbering machines ahead of me, my progress would be slowed to such an extent that I wouldn't make Moscow before nightfall, and that didn't bear thinking about; either that or I would simply suffocate amid the filth pouring out of those straining engines, a noxious potion channelled through the exhausts with every dab of the throttle.

For miles I saw nothing but black smoke and wheels as I launched the Ninja alongside another roaring behemoth, pounding up and down the gears in a bid to maintain maximum torque and minimise the time spent in the danger zone.

I remember thinking, 'Speed is your ally here, your only friend. Get ahead of the fuckers and stay there.' I felt like Sisyphus astride a bolt of green lightening as the Kawasaki hurtled into the turbulent airflow of another clattering trailer, indicator flashing furiously and panniers flapping excitedly as we bounced over the shredded carcass of another huge tyre. But the convoy is never-ending.

I want to stop, if only to rest and breathe, but I know that if I do, all my hard work will be undone; everything I have passed so far will again be in front of me. So I ride on and the miles barely seem to register on the dial.

Eventually, the Ninja's near empty petrol tank forces me to pull in and take a break, and by then I am no longer concerned about lost ground. There is no point worrying because I have realised that there will always be more trucks; there will never be a time when I am at the front of the line, never a moment when my view of Russia isn't encumbered by the rusty, mud-splattered rear of a juggernaut.

At the petrol station I think about lunch, but the food is not appetising. We are in the middle of nowhere and what resides on the plate of the solitary customer is not something I want inside me. It looks like it was once meat, but now it is some new substance, on the brink of becoming a fluid but resisting with cloying tenacity.

I grab a Snickers and fill up, checking the pump repeatedly to ensure I'm putting in some form of petrol. 'Devyanosto pyaty' is what I have been told to look for; I think it means unleaded petrol, but as long as it's not diesel I don't care. Before I left, in a moment of level-headedness, I made a list of the words 'petrol' and 'diesel' in all the languages I expected to encounter. It's worth its weight in gold (considerably more, actually, because being a single sheet of A4, it doesn't weigh much). The fuel is of good quality and I brim the Kawasaki with Super 98.

Then it's back into the madness; another 100 miles where the only respite from the monotony is the ever-present fear of death. Occasionally the trees give way to rows of houses, shacks really, wooden constructions with rusty roofs. Are they 20 years old or 200? It's impossible to tell. Some are clearly derelict, others well-tended with neat gardens. It's odd; who would live out here? As far as I can tell there is nothing to do but leave.

When the road narrows and the houses close in I assume I'm in a town of sorts, although there's little else to suggest it. At a petrol station I stop to stretch my legs. As I walk around, sipping Coke and marvelling at the desolation I pass a big septic tank full of festering matter. It stinks. I look from it to the road and think of the distance I still have to cover, then I look back at the tank; it's like a rancid metaphor: today has been one big shitbox. Moscow had better be worth it. I leave the petrol station on foot and walk along the street, keen to experience

Hostel Napoleon – Moscow: wonder if the little fella's still there?

something of this odd place, even if that is just finding out its name. But I've barely gone 100 metres when a big dog leaps up from behind a fence and starts snarling at me. I have been vaccinated against almost every form of disease known to man; for a while I was practically a walking bio-weapon. But I skipped the rabies shot which could have been designed with this specific animal in mind, so I hurry back to the Ninja and ride off, feeling stupid.

About 50 miles outside the capital the traffic grinds to a halt. Moscow is famous for its monster traffic jams and I fear I may be about to experience one first-hand. It's already 8pm; if I really am stuck in a 50-mile tailback, I see no reason why I won't still be here tomorrow morning.

In front of me, the trucks pant and wheeze as they release the pressure building in their air brakes; they are inching along, and at this speed their enormous bulk is even more apparent. I'm in an tight alleyway formed of gigantic wheels; there's no space to squeeze through even if I wanted to, which I don't, because I'm very aware of the horrible consequences should I misjudge a gap, and snare one of my panniers on the low-hanging trailers of these unforgiving brutes.

If I were to fall here I would be crushed like an egg amid a herd of grazing buffalo. The bike is fully loaded and far too heavy to lift on my own, even if there were space to do so, and, up in their cabs, the drivers can't see me in their mirrors: I doubt they'd notice as the rear wheels of their trailers mangled the Kawasaki into a crumpled mess. But I would, because unless I was very lucky, I'd be an intrinsic part of an ugly green tangle of bars and limbs. So I creep along at a pace dictated by the ebb and flow of the vehicles in front, stealing any opportunity to relax for a few seconds, resting my elbows on my tank-bag, cupping my chin in my hands and watching the temperature gauge rise on the Ninja.

Then, I notice a new form of madness to my right. Drivers are refusing to accept their predicament, and are taking to the hard shoulder to pass the stationary vehicles in front. But there is no hard shoulder, not in the traditional sense, anyway; instead, there is grass and pebbles and mud, but that doesn't stop the 4x4s and the battered BMWs veering off the road and scrambling over the verge to gain a few precious metres where they can. More and more, I see drivers risking all in a bid to make up the slightest ground, and I begin to realise just how bad this jam is. The people taking the risks have been here before; they have spent their evenings choking on smog and inching toward their homes, knowing that if they're lucky they might just make it in time to turn around and head straight back out into the fray. Familiarity breeds contempt, but contempt is too small a word for the emotions on display here on the outskirts of Moscow. This is desperation city, and I realise that unless I am to spend my visit staring at number plates, I must adopt the Russian way.

So I clunk the Kawasaki into gear and try to remember to breathe as I thread my way slowly forward. I'm only 30 per cent sure this will end well; the traffic is so unpredictable that a shunt of sorts seems inevitable. The margins are tiny and the penalties so high, but I know now that I have no choice, and as the metres gradually turn into miles that belief is confirmed. Simply waiting for this mess to resolve itself is not an option.

So I ride on, clipping wing mirrors, trying to apologise without losing my focus, aware that with every mile I push my luck that bit further.

Like most cities, once you're on a ring-road you're just a passenger along for the ride. It's like being caught in the gut of some huge, insatiable monster, squeezing through constipated intestines and hoping you make it to freedom without spending too long in the arse.

It's an unpleasant analogy, but one that seems wholly appropriate as night falls and the bright lights of the Russian capital still seem so far away. It takes another hour before side roads appear like tributaries off a sewer and the accompanying junctions introduce yet more problems. Until now, I'd only worried about crashing into something or being hit from behind, but when a side impact is narrowly avoided I quickly learn not to place too much faith in the convention of traffic lights.

The madness never ends, it only changes form: from the chaotic arterial funnel of the M10 to the hopeless free-for-all of the inner-city, there is danger everywhere and nobody seems to care what they hit. Many cars lack panels, others are bent and mangled, but why bother with repairs when another shunt lies just around the corner?

It's gone 10pm when I arrive at the Hostel Napoleon. I have been riding for 13 hours; for the last four of those nothing has registered beyond the immediate threat of the traffic. But I have made it and I am practically feverish with tension and nervous energy.

Inside the hostel words are streaming out of my mouth and the chap at the reception desk looks confused. But I can't stop; the relief at having survived this horrible day is overwhelming. My notes that evening are succinct, but do justice to my state of mind:

"Was it jubilation I felt when I arrived here? Is that why I was babbling? No, it was the terror gabber. Enough, goodnight."

7

Ground zero

When I set out to ride to Moscow even I wasn't sure I'd make it. It was a challenge that I dreamt up for no good reason, and then felt compelled to at least attempt. It is suggestive of a mental defect: a failure of some rational element of the brain. I have read of such things; a fissure in the cellular dam, resulting in a fundamental breach should the slightest wave of stupidity wash up against it. The resultant flow overwhelms much of the cerebral cortex, and practically decimates key components, like the suicide synapse. And then you find yourself standing in the middle of Red Square, wondering what the fuck you are doing there.

Nikolskaya Street is very beautiful, a giddy mixture of architecture that appears incandescent in the early morning sunshine. I walk up and down it twice, partly to appreciate the ornate splendour of the buildings, but mainly to get my bearings. Moscow is huge, absolutely enormous and despite my hostel being in the centre of the city, I still struggle to determine exactly whereabouts I am in relation to that most obvious reference point – the Kremlin.

But as I walk a little further on, the street bends gently to the right, revealing a tall tower with pretty white windows that could have been plucked from a children's book of fairy tales. Its walls are a rich shade of red and it is topped with a delicate green copper spire. It looks impressive, but only because the building to its right is not yet visible. As I get closer, and the massive sepia walls that surround the citadel close in to dominate my view, I'm struck by a strange sense of familiarity. Despite its distance, this place has been a constant throughout my life, forever on the news in my childhood, associated first with the terrors of nuclear war, then later as the Soviet empire collapsed, representing the poignant beauty of a failed dream; a proud mother, weeping quietly as her children fell around her. To my right, the enormous blocky facade of the State Historical Museum looms up like a bad game of Tetris, dwarfing the spire-topped tower to its left and filling me with excitement. Then I spot the building

The beautiful Nikolskaya Street.

The imposing facade of the State Historical Museum.

St Basil's Cathedral, Red Square.

that represents the end of the road, the culmination of a selfish dream which began almost 3000 miles ago in Crystal Palace. St Basil's Cathedral is bathed in morning sunlight, a vibrant, radiant masterpiece of twirling colours and conical exuberance.

The old Crystal Palace burnt to the ground in 1937, in a conflagration visible across eight counties. It stood for barely 80 years, and now nothing remains but a few headless statues and its huge foundations.

But Red Square has survived many centuries and many eras: it has witnessed war and revolution; execution and coronation; tears of joy and tears of despair have dripped onto its stones, and time has dried them all with indifference. Tsars and communists have marched across its length, brimming with arrogance and power as they strode toward disaster. And today, a hapless biker is joining the millions who have stood in reverential silence in the shadow of so much history.

I sat for a while outside the gigantic GUM department store, which occupies one entire side of Red Square. Some big event was taking place and a huge makeshift arena had been erected to the right of St Basil's Cathedral, where a military band was rehearsing with gusto. Orthodox melodies rang out from the trombones and tubas, crashing awkwardly into loud pop music blasting from a huge PA on the other side of the Square, where gymnasts on horseback were practicing their routines.

I couldn't have arrived at a weirder moment. A string version of Nirvana's *Smells Like Teen Spirit* battled to establish itself over the pomp of the Russian brass.

Hapless-ski.

Young children in traditional dress leapt from stallions that trotted around a ready-made paddock directly in front of Lenin's mausoleum.

I sipped at my coffee and wondered aloud: "Is this all for me?" I could think of no other reason for this grand festival to be occurring at the very moment of my arrival. It seemed somewhat over the top, but I was grateful nonetheless and felt bad for interrupting their rehearsals. They would surely prefer I came back later to enjoy the show proper, so I finished my drink and took a long walk over the Bolshoy Moskvoretskiy Bridge, from where I glimpsed my first uninterrupted view of the Kremlin in its entirety. The red walls tail off into the distance along the bank of the river, and from within, huge golden domes sit atop serene white palaces. It is like some walled utopia that the city's residents may know only from afar. Which I guess it was, until relatively recently.

Once over the bridge, I found myself in a very different Moscow to the polished

Job done.

The impressive ceiling of the GUM department store: scene of one of Russia's most epic battles.

Equestrian display in Red Square, held, I assumed, in my honour.

elegance of the tourist area. Here was the gritty reality of a city home to almost 12 million people. If St Petersburg is the jewel in the Russian crown – gleaming, tidy, clean and elegant – then Moscow is the forge where the blacksmiths toil: hot, very busy, and quite claustrophobic in its intensity.

I struggled to cross roads comprising six or eight lanes, once finding myself in a near fatal game of real-world Frogger. The cars, like the buildings, were an odd mix of the very old, dirty, battered and struggling, and the brand new: pristine luxury machines reflecting the influx of new money that has poured into the city in recent decades, albeit at the expense of the embryonic democracy that Gorbachev kick-started and which Yeltsin stood by and watched crumble from the haze of his private bar.

But that is for the Russians to worry about; for now at least.

In the tunnels of Moscow's exquisite underground railway I quickly discovered I was hopelessly out of my depth. Buoyed by my success in St Petersburg I'd decided to use the metro to visit the monument to Yuri Gagarin in the south of the city. Stalin got a lot of things very wrong, but his vision for the metro led to an extraordinary environment where commuters battle for every last inch of space among marble walls,

Where did it all go wrong? Lenin looks out ...

... over the Moscow of his nightmares.

beautiful statues and pristine ceilings from which hang ornate chandeliers. There could not be a more profound contrast to the grim confines of Tottenham Court Road station anywhere in the world.

But despite its incredible elegance, I found the system almost impossible to navigate. It took the help of some very patient people for me to eventually find my way back to the Kremlin, where I spent the next few hours wandering round in awe, the skin on my jaw wearing thin as it scraped along the floor.

One of the joys of being hopelessly unprepared is the almost constant flow of surprise that awaits you as you experience the world through eyes not pre-loaded with expectation. Everything is there to be seen on TV or through a computer screen; but exploring the world through digital media diminishes the impact when you meet it face-to-face. I had no idea that within the walls of the Kremlin there stood a host of magnificent cathedrals, each of such sublime character as to justify a visit to the city by itself. Palaces too occupy this extraordinary space, which feels almost Disney-like in its perfection. But nothing here is plastic, and the only costumes on display are those worn by the armed guards who are not there to entertain.

The Moscow Metro, not to be confused with London's Northern Line.

Changing of the guard at the Tomb of the Unknown Soldier, outside the Kremlin.

I hadn't expected to be so overwhelmed by this place; it was just a destination; an end-point on a long road, but it is achingly beautiful and I realise that in making this journey I've taken so much for granted. The distance, the roads, the wonderful cities and towns, I've approached all of it with a sort of blinkered arrogance that has bitten me countless times in the last few weeks and humbled me in equal measure. And I took for granted how much I would miss Amy. As I gazed at the beauty on display all around me, I was saddened to the point of tears that my wife wasn't there to share the experience.

I spent a long time among the palaces and the cathedrals and the lovely gardens of the Kremlin, amazed at how peaceful such an enormous tourist attraction could be. Later, I made my way back across Red Square until I stood under the great multi-coloured spiral domes of St Basil's cathedral. It is without doubt one of the three most extraordinary buildings I have ever seen, on a level podium with the Sagrada Familia in Barcelona and New York's doomed Twin Towers. Inside, the space is dark and the corridors narrow. Unlike any other cathedral I have been to, this is not one large, grandiose room full

Serene and tranquil – the walls of the Kremlin keep the madness of Moscow at bay.

of ostentation and extravagance; rather, it consists of nine separate churches, joined together via tight passages.

As I moved between the beautifully decorated chambers, I managed to catch half a conversation between an elderly English couple. I hadn't had a proper chat in days so I introduced myself and we nattered on for a while about this and that. The old fellow had last visited Moscow in 1989 and described a Red Square which I struggled to reconcile with the polished extravagance outside.

Neither the Kazan Cathedral nor the Resurrection Gate were standing at that time, both having been demolished by Stalin to allow large military vehicles to enter the square unimpeded (they were rebuilt in the 1990s). I was amazed to discover that the glamorous GUM department store, with its lavish interior and luxurious products, had once been the scene of a most unlikely conflict: the chap recalled how, upon his last visit, a large wooden table had been placed outside the run-down store, piled high with, of all things, women's lingerie. He remembered mature Russian ladies delving into this ungodly array of garments and struggling fiercely to keep hold of any that took their fancy.

How different the Moscow of 30 years ago must have been, and how unlikely such radical change must have seemed at the time. Our world, forged in stone and metal, appears to us a solid thing, an everlasting tribute to our conceit and pride. The notion of change confounds that arrogance; we strive to deny it, our shoulders pressed firm against the door, refusing entry to that most unwanted visitor. But change is a practiced intruder, and time comes along for the ride. Churchill knew it: when the Crystal Palace burnt down he described it as "the end of an era." How impossible that must have seemed to the men and women who knew nothing but that wonderful structure atop Sydenham

Hill. But it happened nonetheless, and one day my memories of Red Square will include the words 'as it used to be.' But still, I hope someone, somewhere will always remember it as that place where old ladies fought for bras.

It was late when I finally left the Square and began the short walk back to the hostel. I passed under the towering arches of the Resurrection Gate, stopping to take a photo of the old men dressed as Lenin and Stalin, posing for the tourists but not sharing in the smiles. These men had grown up under communism, standing in bread lines while the rest of the developed world queued for colour TVs and video recorders. Now they dressed in the costumes of those bastards who had ruined their lives and those of countless millions, re-packaging the socialist ideal as a cartoon snapshot for the Facebook generation.

Near the Hostel Napoleon I stopped for a final drink and watched a man cross

Lenin and Stalin keep the tourists happy.

An epic city – wonderful, insane, captivating – just don't drive there.

himself as he passed one of the many gold-domed churches that are as common as ATMs on Moscow's streets. They take their religion seriously here: seemingly busy men and women always finding the time to stop and offer up a small prayer as they go about their business.

If I lived here I would pray, too. It's hard to be an atheist on Russia's roads.

Escape

It felt more like fleeing than leaving. The sun was just on the rise as I crawled out of my bunk and began dragging my belongings down to the bike, which was parked in a rat-infested alleyway behind the hostel. One of the 'guests' had gone haywire during the night, drinking himself into a coma and collapsing onto the bed beneath mine. If my alarm hadn't woken me, the foul stench coming from his jeans would have done the trick: too much cheap vodka and some explaining to do when the others wake up. But soiled trousers aren't my concern, not

yet, anyway. I have a long ride ahead of me as I begin the return leg of the journey, and I am full of trepidation.

No, not trepidation. Fear. I am consumed by fear as I strap on the panniers and fidget with bungee cords that are as reluctant to begin this journey as I am. My time in St Petersburg and Moscow has been tarnished by a gnawing dread at the prospect of returning to those horrible roads. I feel as though luck has played a huge part in my still being alive; at some point it has to run out. It is the law of averages, the turning of the great wheel, which seems a fitting metaphor but does little to ease my mind.

So I leave Moscow at first light, before the arteries have time to clog with traffic; giving myself half a chance of surviving at least this first hour or so. But as I come to a stop at a large junction I spot the shattered remains of another bike out of the corner of my eye. It's a crumpled mess dribbling fluids, and the rider is much the same. The ambulance hasn't arrived yet, but it will be

The sun rising behind me can only mean one thing – I'm heading home.

necessary; the helmeted figure is still down, moving but with little confidence. The car parked next to the wreck is barely scratched.

It's another reminder, as if I needed it, that the big impact is just a careless glance away.

The first 150 miles are too easy. I'm out of Moscow proper by 9am and on the M9 heading toward Latvia by 10am. The road is quiet, well paved; I lift my visor to let the cold morning air blow across my face. Was all that worry for nothing? It seems that way as I pull off the road for petrol and stop next to what I realise is the new Russian Grand Prix circuit, the Moscow Raceway. For a petrol-head like myself, this should be an exciting encounter, but I know before I even look that this is just another insipid go-kart track, bereft of challenge, where the vast swathes of run-off allow drivers to get away with sloppy mistakes.

The world has too many of these; there are only three great circuits left: Pikes Peak, the TT Mountain course, and the original Nürburgring; and today's big name racers wouldn't touch any of them with a very long barge pole. Too dangerous, too fast, too much of a throwback to a time when glory meant more than salary. These days our gladiators like the odds stacked a little more in their favour; their fights a little less brutal. In this safety-conscious age, the tigers have been de-clawed, the spears blunted, and the coliseums draped in catch-fencing.

There aren't too many genuine heroes left, and most of them can be found on the Isle of Man every June, risking all for the thrill of it and very little more. John McGuinness, Michael Dunlop, Guy Martin, Conor Cummins; there are others, but most people will never know of them. Men and women who live so close to the edge that life becomes an incandescent glow, framed between hedgerows and walls and houses. That's what they are chasing as they hurtle down Bray Hill, scream past the Bungalow, vanish over the Mountain Mile: it's life, not champagne, which tastes so good when their race is run.

It takes another hour or so before the motorway vacates the urban sprawl and now I'm riding along a deep scar that cuts a neat line through the forest. The morning sun is casting shadows ahead of me, and I enjoy the novelty of heading west for the first time in weeks. Latvia by mid-afternoon seems a distinct possibility, but then Russia throws a curveball and everything turns to shit.

I pass a signpost that indicates roadworks ahead and my limbs stiffen with anxiety. I stop at traffic lights and the workmen eye me cautiously. They know what lies ahead and are wondering how long it will be before they hear the distant wail of ambulance sirens. For a moment I can scarcely believe what I see: the road has gone. Not the M9 – that continues for many, many miles – but the surface of it, the bit that differentiates it from the grass and rocks each side, that bit is no longer there. I look ahead, expecting to see it reappear a few metres further on, sure this rocky patch must be an inconvenient break in the asphalt. But there is only more of the same, stretching into the distance like a filthy old carpet. This huge motorway, the equivalent of the UK's M1, has abruptly turned into a single lane, rock-strewn path for which neither I, nor my motorcycle, are prepared.

None of the workmen will return my gaze; they glance in my general direction but they are not about to chat. Even if they spoke English, they could offer nothing in the way of hope. They would only be able to confirm my worst fears: that this catastrophe is what now passes for the motorway.

I can't ride the Ninja over this: it is literally loose rock and pebble. There is nothing that won't move when the tyres grind over it and the bike would struggle

The bollards indicate the edge of the road; well, something has to.

even if it weren't weighed down with all my possessions. But there is no alternative. To the best of my knowledge there is no other route out of here and even if there were, I have no means of finding it. Returning to Moscow is neither a realistic nor a welcome prospect, because that would put me on the path back to St Petersburg and I never ever want to see the M10 again.

There is nothing for it but to push on and hope that when the suspension inevitably collapses or the tyres explode I am able to bounce out of harm's way.

The lights turn to green and behind me the trucks grunt and wheeze as their drivers ignore my predicament and squeeze past, firing tiny rocks out of their deep-treaded tyres. I follow at a distance and at a painfully slow pace that means I am always in somebody's way. If I exceed 10mph the crunch that accompanies the suspension bottoming out is as painful to my ears as it is to my lower back, but behind me the trucks are pushing on; they have targets and quotas to meet and there is no room on this crumbling path for sympathy. In fact, there is no room for anything but the trucks, which occupy the entire width of the road, leaving no space even to get out of their way.

This is madness on another level and now this single lane is home to vehicles travelling in both directions. Through the dust kicked up by those massive trailers I can make out a wagon heading directly toward me. The

Pretty soon the rubble on the edge of the road became the road.

truck is consuming every last inch of road; there is no hard shoulder, only a thick bank of mud that defines this ludicrous path. That is where I end up, struggling to hold the bike as we come to an abrupt stop in this semi-quagmire.

For the next couple of hours I simply try and survive, which shouldn't be difficult on a major arterial road in a developed country, but here is as close to impossible as you can get and live to tell the tale.

If any road that lacks a surface can be said to have a redeeming feature, it is the M9's merciful lack of traffic. Had the flow been half as bad as that which I'd encountered between Moscow and St Petersburg, I really don't think it would have been possible to continue. As it was, the passing cars and trucks were at least separated by moments of calm; minutes of solitude that lasted just long enough for the choking dust clouds to subside before another leviathan commenced its attack.

I lost track of everything as I bounced along that road. Time, distance, location, fuel; none of it registered. It was simply a lesson in endurance that eventually left me in a sort of catatonic stupor. I was so sure that the bike or the tyres would eventually fail that I stopped worrying about it. I just rode on, absolutely convinced that at some point I would need serious help, which I

The poor Kawasaki did not sign up for this.

Near Latvia, I brim the Ninja with quality 98 fuel, as a sort of thank-you.

would deal with when the time came. But it never did. That 11-year old Kawasaki just kept going, its fairing creaking with every jolt, its forks soaking up the pain, and its rider utterly resigned to failure.

When the road briefly returned and I was able to stop and inspect the damage, I was gob-smacked. There was none. The seals weren't leaking, the Michelins hadn't lost a single pound of pressure, the suspension rebounded firmly when I pressed against it. A sports bike on road tyres should not be able to withstand that sort of abuse, not relentlessly, hour upon hour.

As I made my way slowly out of Russia, the thing that should have been the road came and went with cruel irregularity. Just when it seemed the worst was over, another sign would introduce more miles of misery, rubble, dust and cursing.

Which was a shame for many reasons, not least because the M9 passes through some quite beautiful countryside that reminded me very much of England. On those infrequent paved stretches of road I tried to calm myself and enjoy the ride, but it was like trying to relax at the dentist; something awful was about to happen and the pleasantries only made things worse.

Eventually, at about 6pm, with the sun still high in the cloudless sky, I saw a signpost that said Latvia was not too far away. The road became as perfect as any I had ridden on, the traffic all but disappeared and Russia tried to pretend that nothing bad had ever happened. But I was not about to be fooled by this cheap deception; the day had bruised me to the core, both physically and mentally, and it would take more than some pleasant hedgerows and a nice stretch of Tarmac to sweep this mean affair under the carpet.

Before I reached the border I stopped and scribbled down some notes, not really thinking about what I was writing but keen to capture the raw emotion I was feeling before time and distance smoothed the jagged edges. What came out was neither fair nor representative; in fact it was a pretty harsh summary of my recent experience. But at the time it seemed like a fitting farewell:

"Fuck you Russia, I am finally free of your crushing embrace. You are a vengeful monster with a heart full of hate and a pretty smile. I have survived, as has the Ninja, but we are forever scarred by your torturous games and we will never return."

As goodbyes go there have been worse, but not many. In hindsight, it saddens me greatly that we didn't part on better terms, but the truth is I was just happy to be out of there, alive and in one piece. At that moment, the kindness and beauty and many delights I had experienced were about as far from my mind as they would ever be. Which is why I needed to write down exactly how I was feeling at that time, so that if I ever again thought that I might like to ride a motorcycle in Russia, I would have no one to blame but myself.

8
Westbound

That's the Latvian border behind me. I've never been
so pleased to see armed guards.

Latvia

Ludza is 20 miles or so from the Latvian/
Russian border, and as I rode along the
sweeping E12, over hills and past pretty
meadows full of late summer flowers, I felt
all the stress and worry and outright fear of
the last 12 hours trickle away like rainwater
off a freshly polished fairing.

My relief at arriving at the border had
been tempered only by a concern that
somewhere along the way I'd failed to get
some form or other registered and that I
would be told to return to Moscow post
haste to collect another stamp. But that
didn't happen. Despite the enormous queue
of lorries waiting at the crossing, the border
experience was relatively simple and not

unduly stressful. It was considerably quieter
and less formal than the entry into Russia
via Finland, although that may have been
because getting out is just easier than getting
in. I don't know and, honestly, I didn't care.

I felt like Houdini casting off his chains.
There would be time to reflect on Russia, to
remember the thrill and excitement of being
somewhere so completely different, but that
would be later, when the final dregs of terror
had dissolved in my veins and my heart had
slowed to a more comfortable rhythm.

In the shower of the Hotel Lucia I
washed away the last traces of that intense
day, which disappeared down the plug hole
in a dark swirling mess of dirt and sweat. As
a final test of my endurance, I discovered on

While leaving Russia I'd been dreaming of the fast, flowing Latvian roads … humph!

my arrival that the entire road around the hotel had been dug up, leaving bare rock and dirt to ride across for the last thirty yards or so to the car park. For a while I thought I might cry, but it was laughter that finally emerged from my dry, cracked lips. Under any other circumstances I would have been horrified at the prospect of taking the Ninja over that rocky little path, but not now; they could have put that hotel on top of a volcano and the Kawasaki would have scaled it without protest. A few more stones and the absence of a street would not stop us, and together we bounced toward the end of a truly hellish day's ride.

In the hotel restaurant, Foreigner's *I Want to Know What Love Is* reminds me that I must call Amy later. But right now I am too absorbed in the menu to do anything but salivate. If my maths are correct – and there is no reason to think they are – nothing on this menu costs more than GBP3, including the spirits. I have not eaten a proper meal for days, partly because I haven't had time, but

mainly because Moscow and St Petersburg are teeming with tourists and the prices are eye-watering. So I go a little crazy, and despite chomping my way through two starters, a huge main, three deserts and a bottle of wine, my bill only just creeps into double figures.

Thrown to the lions at the Hotel Lucia.

Getting it wrong at Druids.

The wall of shame.

The next morning is bright and sunny and after a full breakfast I leave the little town of Ludza a happy and contented soul. I am so looking forward to a gentle day's ride under a clear blue sky, down through Rēzekne, toward Daugavpils and then into Lithuania. But even before I'm past Rēzekne I'm worried. The roads are horrible; not Russian horrible, but pretty awful nonetheless. Immediately my optimism and ebullience begin to wane. I hadn't realised how close to the great chasm of despair I had strayed, but it quickly becomes apparent that my resolve is very low indeed. I tell myself to chin-up; this is just a small road, it will improve, the scenery is beautiful, the weather perfect: 'This is your adventure, Turner,' I tell myself sternly, 'and you better make the most of it because it sure as hell will seem like a good deal in six months' time when you're back at work and staring into another winter's morning.'

That does the trick. I lift my visor, breathe in the fresh, crisp air and force a smile. In a bid to lighten my mood, I think back to some of the wonderful times I've had since passing my motorcycle test. Dawdling round the Nürburgring on that first tentative wet lap; finding the gravel trap at Druids just as I thought I was getting the hang of Brands Hatch; the many long motorway miles en route to far off destinations, the excitement and thrill of arrival and the frustration and resignation of being hopelessly lost again.

It was barely ten years ago that I was pottering round the test centre on my little Honda CG125, unknowingly in the process of opening so many doors I didn't even realise were closed. One-by-one I learned to cross car parks, cities, counties and countries.

In the Pyrenees I learned to trust my tyres and carry that little bit more speed into a bend, pushing my own comfort zone if not that of the bike; coming down from the Alps, I discovered the value of the rear brake; somewhere in the south of France I lifted the front wheel for the first time, and carried the grin, if not the wheelie, back to England. It was Brands again where my knee slider first made contact with Tarmac (not entirely unrelated to my later encounter with the gravel trap) and in the mountains above Corfu I shared the final, poignant moments in the life of a 250 Suzuki.

Looking back on those years, it seemed that every ride was full of discovery and excitement. There was never a boring moment, no matter how uninspiring the road or the destination. I think that's still largely true. A motorbike, ridden enthusiastically, can transform even the most mundane journey into a greater thrill than many people will experience in a lifetime.

I've also met a lot of great people through motorcycling, notably motor racing legend Murray Walker who sent me a delightful letter after I ambushed him with a copy of my first book at the Goodwood Revival (I say delightful letter, I mean restraining order ...)* But with a few notable exceptions, much of my riding has been done alone, which is the way I like it.

A motorcycle is many things to many people, but there are very few bikers who won't tell you that in some small way their machine represents a means of escape; and we all need to escape now and again. Some people do so by lying on a beach for two weeks, slowly roasting; others retreat into online worlds where goblins and knights and princesses provide a sense of purpose painfully absent in the real world of offices and managers and spreadsheets. And then there are those for whom 'escape' is just a synonym for 'ride;' whether that's cruising along Route 66 on a fully-dressed Hog, or launching off the Mountain at Cadwell Park, it all boils down to the same essential desire. And that explains, at least partially, why I am now in Latvia, riding my trusty Kawasaki

*He sent me a lovely reply telling me, among others things, of his father's victories at the Nürburgring; it remains a very cherished possession.

over a road which is not improving as I had hoped, but is rather deteriorating with every painful mile.

I try to ignore the constant clattering of the suspension, which is being pounded remorselessly and channelling a not inconsiderable amount of the punishment up through the forks and into my wrists. It's like holding on to a jackhammer, but we are going forward, not down, at least for the time being. At a crossroads I gamble on a left turn. The road can't be any worse and for a few miles it isn't – although it's no better either – but then I see a sign for roadworks and my heart practically stops. It is inconceivable that the Latvians would be so mean as to replicate the Russian way. Surely no other nation would be as hopelessly misguided as to simply remove the road while they repair it?

But that is exactly what they have done, and as I guide the Ninja once again over a surface best described as lunar, I feel all of that hope and optimism that had accompanied me as I left the hotel fall away, to be crushed among the stones and rocks below.

The non-road lasts for about six miles, during which it follows the Russian example almost perfectly. It abruptly filters into a single lane, where traffic from both directions attempts to force its way through gaps that simply don't exist. Red lights mean nothing out here; I follow a bus and a van with Latvian plates through a stop signal thinking they must know best, and the next minute we are all swerving off the road as a truck comes blasting toward us. Back home this would make the local news.

I never expected this kind of ordeal, never expected that I would have to ride for mile after mile on shards of broken rock as big as water melons. This is what happens in Africa. Of course, I should have researched all this before I left, but I probably wouldn't

have come if I'd known how bad things would get. That's another advantage of this foolhardy approach to travel; there is no greater obstacle than fear, and I am a fearful person. I do not enjoy danger; I don't thrill at its proximity. It is better not to know, to plunge headlong into the dark waters thinking only of the refreshing chill and not the sharks circling beneath.

They say there is nothing to fear but fear itself, which is true, but only up to a point: it is perfectly natural to shudder at the sight of a huge bat or a very sinister child. Confront fear head-on and it will almost certainly win. So I choose to ignore it, or turn a blind eye to its causes, and then I find myself on a dirt-track in Latvia riding through a dust cloud into the path of a massive truck.

Eventually, the road surface does return, but my attitude toward the whole country has hopelessly soured. I no longer have the strength to endure this craziness; to see the light amid the darkness. The excitement that had once spurred me on has been exhausted by so many relentless miles in the saddle. I need to stop, to re-charge my batteries, but I don't have time. If I want a job to return to I need to press on. I'm still about 2,000 miles from home and as much as I want to enjoy the ride, the worry that accompanies these dirt-track miles is clouding my mind. If the bike falls apart I couldn't blame it, but it would be a massive blow. It has performed so well, handled everything that's been thrown at it, but each day now I'm making ever-more unreasonable demands of it. I feel like I'm whipping a stallion into the grave, but I just want to get to a place where the roads go the distance and aren't merely interludes among gravel.

As I head further south things do improve, but not enough to change my jaundiced perception of a country I had placed my faith in. I feel let down by Latvia, which is stupid but reflects my state of mind.

I think it means 'no speed limits' ... ahem.

I needed an easy day and this was supposed to be it, but so far it's been another chore. Still, the countryside that I ride through is beautiful; agricultural but not on an industrial scale, it is as I image England was between the wars.

I stop for petrol and grab some fruit and crisps. With some food in my belly I begin to perk up a little, reminding myself that my problems are all of my own making, and that under different circumstances this country could be almost idyllic. It's an impression affirmed when I ride past an old

man wearing overalls and a grubby white cap; he is perched on the back of a wooden cart that is being pulled along by a sturdy old horse. The man looks happy, the horse is trotting contentedly; there is no urgency to be found in this scene and it cheers me enormously. I wave and he smiles and nods a greeting and I feel a little lump rise in my throat. It's a perfect moment which comes out of nowhere and lifts the spirits like a friendly embrace.

Approaching Daugavpils I suddenly realise I haven't been paying the slightest

Authentic Latvia; a beautiful country emerging into a strange, new world.

attention to where I am or which way I should be going. I've been riding along in a sort of somnambulant daze now that the road has improved, and there is nothing to keep me alert, save for the occasional village with its old shops and even older women. In the centre of the town I pull in to a supermarket car park because I am very lost. I'm sure the Lithuanian border is no more than 20 miles away, but I can't see any signposts indicating which road I should take, so once again I rely on the kindness of strangers and once again the world proves it is full of wonderful people.

There aren't many folk around, save for an old fellow who is staring at me with an expression of bemused interest. He won't speak any English, that's obvious from his age and attire. I don't feel the slightest unease about making such assumptions; I'm not judging him, any less than I would be if I assumed he couldn't fly. It's a fair call with no hidden malice and it proves correct, but he is keen to help. I explain where I am heading and, at the mention of Lithuania, he begins pointing in big sweeping gestures that are about as useful as his words. He stabs at the air, points left and right, makes bridge symbols with his hands, but we both know this isn't working. I can see that he's getting irritated at his inability to convey meaning, and that makes me feel guilty: I am the fool in this picture, not he. Then another, younger man comes out of the store and they start chatting and gesticulating. The younger fellow speaks good English and through him his father finds a conduit to channel his frustration. The son laughs at his father's irritation and explains to me what the old man is trying to say.

The border is not far, but the road I require is on the other side of a river and around an awkward one-way system. My confusion must be apparent because the young man turns and speaks quickly to his dad, who nods approvingly and squeezes into the back of their car.

"I think it is easier if you follow me," says the young chap. I'd been hoping for this because their instructions were mind-boggling, but still I feel a little guilty at almost manipulating their assistance.

"You're sure?" I say with as little conviction as possible.

"Of course, it's not too far anyway and I think perhaps you may not find it on your own."

He is right. I think without their assistance I should have resigned myself to living out the rest of my days in Daugavpils. But finally, after about half an hour, their little red car pulls over and the younger of the two men hops out.

"Just carry on now, straight this way and you will reach the border in maybe five kilometres."

I thank him as best I can and wave my gratitude through the rear window to where his father is sitting with a big grin on his face. They don't seem in the slightest perturbed at having driven so far out of their way. I think perhaps helping people is almost as good as being helped, although I can't honestly say this is why I repeatedly get so lost, as a benevolent gift to the world.

But as I ride past the empty border into Lithuania and Latvia disappears from view, I realise how stupid I have been in allowing such trite difficulties to influence my perception of a wonderful country. It is easily done, especially after the challenges of recent days, but these are excuses, nothing more. Latvia has taught me a valuable lesson and I realise again how lucky I am.

Lithuania

There is no physical border between Latvia and Lithuania, and in truth, there is no need for one. The difference is like night and day, and, as I crossed into Lithuania, I was left in no doubt that a change had occurred. Lithuania has money and Latvia does not, and that makes for a very profound contrast. It was as though I'd passed through an invisible curtain, behind which lay a gleaming, polished, tidy example of what Latvia could one day become. The last few miles had been along an ill-maintained rural road, very quiet and lined with tall grass and empty bottles. Occasionally a car would zoom past and a crisp packet or cigarette butt would emerge from the window and come tumbling back along the road toward me; it felt like what it was: a transitional zone that no one cared about because, one way or another, it wouldn't be their problem for much longer.

But at Zarasai, a couple of miles over the border, where I stopped next to a huge and very beautiful lake, the cars were clean and dent-free. The people moved without that stumped hustle that comes with too many years of physical toil, and the old buildings were well maintained and charming.

I felt like I'd taken a huge step toward a world I was familiar with, and as much as that should have saddened me as a traveller, it delighted me as a motorcyclist. At the edge of the lake, a wonderful twirling bridge swooped out over the waters, offering an uncluttered view of a splendid panorama consisting of lush forests and calm waters, in the reflection of which bumbling white clouds ambled across the blue sky above.

It was exactly as I thought Latvia would be, and I suspect will be in a few years' time

Lithuania: a polished version of Latvia, thanks to EU money.

This bridge snakes out over the lake at Zarasai.

"I'll bite your legs off!" Not sure if this really had anything to do with Monty Python.

when the tourists realise how pretty and cheap it is. But riding through Lithuania was a joy, not an effort: mile after mile of gently undulating, smooth roads and beautiful scenery; the perfect place to go motorbiking.

My route through Lithuania was direct, taking me down through Ukmergė and Kaunas toward Marijampolė, across endless miles of pleasant rolling countryside. Now and again I'd pass a large village or town, where ugly concrete relics of the communist age still stood like miserable martyrs to a lost cause. Decrepit tower blocks, once white, now tumorous grey with shit-coloured stains dripping from the ironwork, mired the landscape like gravestones – a grim reminder of a past that no one could call a success.

Latvia and Lithuania seem destined to go the same way as Prague and Kraków; their cheapness and natural beauty making them ideal tourist destinations for happy-go-lucky Westerners who want to drink themselves into oblivion in a different bar each night. The communist chic only adds to the charm. Why not? The populations of these beleaguered nations deserve something for all the years of hardship. Russia is either ignoring, removing, or turning its history into a tourist attraction. How long before these tiny nations follow suit? Cheap booze and stag parties and a free Hammer and Sickle badge with every visit.

Kaunas seemed a pretty if rather frantic city, but the prospect of riding around for hours trying to find accommodation, getting dreadfully lost and hopelessly frustrated, outweighed the appeal of discovery, so I pushed on toward Marijampolė in the hope of finding a quiet and relaxing campsite in which to spend the night.

In Sasnava, which sits just off the E67 on the fringes of Marijampolė, I followed signs depicting either a tent or a port-a-loo, knowing that I wouldn't be disappointed

Soviet iconography in Latvia – the memories linger as the country looks west to its future..

either way. The village was tiny and the 'campsite' merely an empty bit of grass next to a playground and a rather grim store. It made me nervous because it reminded me of too many cheap horror films where naive travellers have been butchered by inbred locals. My fears increased when I discovered the reception area smelled of meat and the only person around was a wizened old hunchback with bloodied hands and a mischievous grin that revealed torn strands of flesh hanging from sharpened teeth. I shook my head vigorously and the image disappeared, leaving a kindly shopkeeper in its wake. She handed me a piece of paper with a phone number on it and told me to call the campsite owner, who spoke good English and soon arrived with a friendly smile and the key to 'the facilities.'

The facilities lay behind a huge metal door which opened on to a large dark room containing a small loo, a hot tub and a pool table. It was very, very odd. The shower was just a space with a plastic sheet across it and there was no hot water; but I didn't mind because I had no intention of showering in there anyway: the place maintained an eerie vibe that was not conducive to my undressing, which would have felt like unwrapping a ready meal.

I splashed some water over my face and made my way back to the tent, thinking that if this evening ended in anything other than my being cremated inside a huge wicker man I should be very surprised. The lady who ran the patch of grass I would call home for the next few hours was chatting to the store-keeper when I returned. She was very friendly and helpful and I felt a little bad for thinking her a cannibal, but now the fear had a hold and I couldn't shake it off. We chatted for a while and she helped me purchase some vegetarian food and a couple of beers, and then, as I was about to leave, she reminded me to keep the key to the

shower room with me in my tent at all times and not to leave. I swallowed heavily. "Don't leave the tent?" I said. "Why not, what will happen to me if I leave the tent?"

"No," she laughed, "don't leave the campsite without returning the key."

"Oh right, of course!" I said with a dismissive wave, "will do."

Then I strolled back to my tent, zipped it shut, padlocked the zip and lay cowering inside my sleeping bag for the next eight hours. I did not sleep well that night.

Poland

There is a small rest area just before the Polish border where two metal characters built out of old car parts stand next to the road and wave inanely at the passing traffic. They are cheerful, optimistic and not a little weird, but they filled me with delight, and, if you asked me for a better abstract of my experience in Lithuania, I would struggle to find one. Poland, however, seemed a more serious proposition from the get go. Perhaps it is the weight of all that recent history which bears down on the country like an anvil on a flower bed, and from which it will never escape.

Whatever the reason, as I rode past the empty white buildings, which I assumed had once been the fixed border crossing, I felt a strange anxiety pass through me. I was conscious of this and trying to understand it when a huge wolf leapt from the verge into the road and bounded across my path. I braked heavily but unnecessarily, because it was gone before I'd have had chance to hit it; but even in that split second, its enormous power and physicality were obvious. It was a huge beast, far bigger than any dog and, under different circumstances, perhaps I wouldn't have been so overjoyed by its fleeting presence. But this extraordinary encounter only confirmed my suspicions that Poland should be approached with

Rather grim and slightly terrifying campsite near the Lithuanian/Polish border.

caution. Fate had fired a warning shot across my bows and I would take no chances in the land of the wild wolf.

With the imprint of that wonderful animal practically burnt onto my retina, I rode on along the E67 waiting excitedly for more drooling beasts to hurl themselves into my path, but sadly that encounter was not to be repeated, and I found myself meandering along a lightly busy road, passing through huge dense pine forests and acres of shimmering cornfields. Many of the towns I passed through appeared tired and dilapidated, the shops old and the pavements cracked; yet they seemed to have ample funds to maintain the fabulous churches that sat resplendent in their centres. In stark contrast, the shabby stores sat like beggars at the feet of a bloated lord.

A quarter of a century after the event and still the fetid air of communism lingers over these places. You can taste it in the diesel fumes and you can see its lingering footprint in the communal flats that could be anywhere in Eastern Europe; an unwelcome guest, reluctant to leave a party that finished decades ago and was never much fun anyway.

But that is only part of the story. The E67 continues on to Warsaw, and between towns offers a delightful insight into the rural aspects of the country. I would have ridden that road all the way back to London if the scenery remained half as pretty and inspiring as it had since leaving Lithuania. Unfortunately, that was not an option. After Warsaw I picked up the E30, which is a motorway in the traditional sense and offers nothing but banality and speed.

When the rain came I pulled off the motorway and headed toward the town of Skierniewice where I'd been told I'd find a campsite, but never did. I looked, believe me I searched practically every inch of that little town, whose residents could be divided between those adamant that a campsite lay just around the corner, and those equally

And good day to you, too, sir: a friendly face on the way out of Lithuania.

confident that there wasn't one to be found within a hundred miles of the place.

A natural optimism encouraged me to pursue the advice of the former, but after I'd wasted about two hours I decided that there may well have been more merit in the words of the latter. So I turned my back on Skierniewice and rode through the forest that occupies so much of the region toward Żyrardów. At that time, Żyrardów held no attraction to me whatsoever, it just happened to be signposted in the direction I was travelling; but the name had a nice ring to it, like it could be the next Lamborghini, so I decided to pay it a visit in the hope of finding cheap accommodation and, equally as important, petrol.

The Ninja is all the bike I could ever wish for. It has been a lime green constant in my life for the best part of a decade. It would have been best man at my wedding if I could have found it a tie that didn't clash with the paint. But it's not perfect; it has a shortcoming that adds a modicum of excitement to the most uneventful of journeys, and that is the absence of a fuel gauge. I doubt the world will ever know for sure why the men and women at Kawasaki decided to omit this most useful of functions. Maybe running out of petrol is cool in Japan? Perhaps Japanese teenagers impress their friends with tales of long walks along motorways carrying empty jerry cans? I don't know and it is not for me to question the customs of the Orient; but it is an annoying oversight nonetheless.

Other than through sad experience, there is no way of knowing when the fuel in the tank is about to expire, although any situation that requires the taps to be fully opened – a reckless overtake or a late blast through an amber traffic light – is pretty much guaranteed to coincide with the final dregs of petrol trickling through the carburettors into oblivion. When that happens the engine immediately dies,

which as any qualified mechanic will tell you, has a dramatic impact on one's forward momentum. As bike and rider slow rapidly and the traffic behind begins to swerve all around, honking furiously and yelling quite inventive abuse, you are forced to begin a procedure so bewilderingly awkward that it must have been devised as a cruel hoax that somehow slipped through the net.

Imagine the following at 90mph on a busy motorway, at night and in the rain, and then explain to me how the same nationality that designed this madcap process managed to develop out of the Stone Age. First, you must reach down behind your left knee – not the most convenient place on a motorcycle – in the hope of locating a dial, about the size of a large coin, which operates the reserve tank. The dial is recessed and turning it would be ponderously difficult even if you weren't wearing thick leather gloves. Assuming by some miracle you have not been squashed by the time you finally locate and grasp it, the dial must then be rotated 180 degrees anti-clockwise, which involves much swearing and the necessary dislocation of your left wrist.

Now you are free to replace both hands on the bars and begin apologising to the chap who moments earlier came close to creating a new type of vehicle, comprising his bonnet and your rear wheel, and who has now pulled alongside you and is bleeding hate in your direction through his side window. At the same time you can begin dabbing the starter switch, which eventually encourages enough fuel into the chambers to allow the plugs to ignite, enabling you to make good your escape and hope that a petrol station has been conveniently placed at some point within the next 30 miles, or thereabouts. Of course, there is no way of knowing exactly how far you will be able to travel on the reserve tank – because there is no fuel

There's a good reason for that spare fuel container.

gauge – but you do at least now have the luxury of knowing that when the engine dies a second time there will be no need to repeat the process, because both tanks will then be empty and you will be well and truly screwed.

Which was exactly how I was feeling as the Ninja's engine spluttered into silence and we began the gradual process of quiet deceleration that would leave me trudging through miles of Polish forest in the hope of finding services. Except that by what can only be described as a genuine miracle, we rolled to a stop quite literally inches from the entrance to the most welcoming petrol station I have ever seen.

Once again the Kawasaki had saved the day and as I pushed it those last few feet onto the forecourt I found myself thanking it repeatedly and praising it enthusiastically, as one might a mountain rescuer who has just plucked some hapless rambler off the side of a Cairngorm in a blizzard. I suspect they have audio on their surveillance cameras in those petrol stations because the lady behind the till looked at me suspiciously as I tried to pay, as though I might start chatting to the cash register or bantering with the coffee machine, but I didn't care. That moment solidified the already well-formed bond between my bike and me. We were a partnership; it was the Millennium Falcon to my Han Solo (or maybe Chewbacca, I hadn't shaved for weeks) and there was nothing in the world I'd rather have been riding. You could have offered me a Lamborghini Żyrardów and I would have turned it down.

Żyrardów

There is a song, recorded by Johnny Cash and Hank Williams Jr, called *That Old Wheel*, which I sing now and again on long empty roads when there's no-one around to hear me butcher it. It's about life's ups and downs, how the wheel turns and we must roll along with it, accepting that today's highs may be tomorrow's lows, and vice-versa. At least that's how I interpret it, it may just be about an errant wheel bouncing down the road, but I like to think there's a little more to it than that. Anyway, that song resonates with me, and never more so than when I'm on a road trip and each day brings with it some little gift or comical misfortune.

As I walked along the pristine, brick-walled corridors of the Aparthotel in Żyrardów, I felt that old wheel had come to rest in a very favourable position. This was luxury I hadn't experienced for some time, and which I had not thought possible earlier that day as I'd ridden miserably around Skierniewice and its neighbouring villages.

The previous night I had slept on a communal lawn just off a motorway, where all of the world's dogs had congregated for a howling contest; now I was standing in the doorway of a hotel room where crisp clean sheets beckoned, and a proper toilet welcomed me with the discrete cordiality of a professional butler. Best of all, two perfectly placed skylights provided a splendid view of the town's beautiful cathedral, which stretched up into the heavens from the square opposite.

I unpacked the two beers which I had carefully stowed in my rucksack earlier that day, collapsed onto the bed and fell sound asleep. The sun had almost set when I woke, and, from my window, the red brickwork of the cathedral seemed to glow warm and fiery in the twilight. I popped the top off one of the bottles and took it with me into the shower, stealing sips under the warm,

artificial rain; 'if only the elements were so easily controlled.'

Leaving the bathroom, I caught sight of myself in the tall mirror and was surprised to see how prominent my ribs had become.   I realised how little I'd been eating, or perhaps, how little I needed to eat in order to feel fine and function well: an apple here, a cheese sandwich there, a banana for breakfast, and the odd bar of chocolate for lunch. I wasn't purposefully limiting my intake, but with the days so full of travel and tents and things to do and see, food had become little more than a necessary interruption. Still, the lack of sustenance, compounded by long days and the physicality of riding a motorcycle and hauling luggage about was clearly taking a toll.

Does travel broaden the mind, or just thin the body?

"Well, at least your fingernails aren't falling out," I said aloud. But my skinny, bearded reflection was already on its way to the bar.

The hotel's corridors were lined with old photographs of Żyrardów, which I was surprised to learn was a relatively modern development. It grew up around a textile factory built by a couple of brothers in the early 19th century. The town is full of lovely, simple brick buildings, the material of choice at the time of its creation. Consequently, it has a unique charm, very different to so many older towns and villages, where the sites of interest are often medieval and built of stone.

Directly outside the hotel I was lured toward a small café by the presence of a slightly dilapidated motorcycle and sidecar. It looked familiar, and, on closer inspection, I was delighted to discover it was a Ural, a Russian-built outfit identical to that which my in-laws, John and Julie, used to own when they were younger.

Żyrardów – another hidden gem, and a truly lucky find.

Lunch, or maybe dinner; probably both. I lost two stone in three weeks.

John told me he purchased his Ural when he saw a similar one with a machine gun mounted on the sidecar in a magazine, and I remember thinking that there couldn't be a better reason for buying a motorcycle than that.

The bike was fenced off from the footpath by a low-slung rope, over which I deftly stepped when no-one was looking, and hopped on-board. As my feet found the pegs and my fingers curled around the bars, I felt an immediate connection with this ancient contraption. It was, after all a motorcycle, despite its odd gear-shifter, flat tyres, and unfamiliar dials and buttons, and as such it felt like home away from home. I always get that feeling no matter what the bike: I felt it the first time I clambered onto the seat of my granddad's BMW, hidden

away in the back of the garage, and I feel it every time I swing a leg over the Kawasaki: that familiar buzz of excitement that seems to linger around these metal beasts like a mystic aura.

I looked down into the empty sidecar and imagined my mother-in-law seated there, semi-frozen despite the many layers of thick jumpers and gloves, barrelling down a snow-lined A5 on a wintery trip from Shrewsbury to London. Could I ever convince Amy that this was a good idea? 'Only if you can find one made of chocolate,' I thought.

As the crow flies

Żyrardów felt like an ending, and I guess in many ways it was. There was still much of Poland left to ride through before I made Germany, but riding through it was exactly

Where's the machine gun? At home on the Ural.

what I would be doing from now on. The last grains of sand were trickling through the hourglass, and time was very much against me. But more than that, my enthusiasm for the adventure had waned; not entirely, I still bristled with excitement each morning, but as the day wore on that fire would fade too quickly, like dying embers flaring momentarily on a passing breeze. And with time now against me, I had to alter my route, prioritising speed over interest and somewhat compromising the spirit of this final leg.

No time now to stop by Prague and reminisce about those teenage days spent drinking cheap absinthe in subterranean bars, talking politics in the park and debating life late into the night. Maybe that was for the best; teenage memories should remain

just that. Prague is a very different place now to those giddy years of the early 90s, when it stood like a naked heroine, the discarded dress of the communist era revealing the perfect contours of an idyllic form, full of youthful hope and optimism. It felt like San Francisco in the '60s, or at least how I've come to image San Francisco felt when the world was turning to shit around it and the squats were full of young idealists, writing and singing and debating a better future that would never come.

We would spend the evenings on the Charles Bridge, jostling for space among the crowds who gathered around our friend, the Brazilian busker, Ise Severo. Ise could work a crowd better than Mick Jagger; he was the most popular street entertainer in Prague at the time by some margin, and

The Ninja makes a friend in the garage of the Aparthotel.

his companionship lent us an undeserved credibility which we milked like acolytes at the resurrection. Later, when the final rasping lyrics of the *Charles Bridge Song* had drifted into the warm night sky and Ise had called time on his set, we would head over to one of the islands on the Vltava and drink and laugh until the sun came up.

If those days still exist, then they are for other, younger people; people with hope in their veins and a simmering anger at the injustice of the world. It dissipates, that anger; it boils down to a slurry of tired cynicism and petty frustrations. That is what we call growing up; but 'giving up' is probably a better phrase.

Ah, but this is the talk of a man whose journey is nearly over, and mine still has some way to go. The next morning I stumble down the corridors of the Aparthotel, dragging my panniers and tent toward my strong and trusty steed, which ticks over patiently on the pavement and attracts the local children like a stray dog.

It growls and they step back as one, open-jawed and wide-eyed. I feel like a comic book hero as I ride away, blipping the throttle to keep the attention of my juvenile admirers. Why not? It is a rare thing in this life to feel like a genuine king, and I will take it when I can, even though my subjects are barely old enough to read.

The sun is shining as I leave Żyrardów, the last outpost of this wild frontier, beyond which lies a recognisable path to a more familiar world, where the signposts make sense and I am just another British biker riding roads too close to home.

Lonely by day; spooky by night – a deserted Helenesee.

Near the German border I camp at Helenesee, a huge sprawling site on the edge of a lake that is as bleak and lonely a place as any I have encountered. I arrive as the remnants of a rock festival are departing. Last night this place was a heaving mess of drunken party-goers, most of whom are now sat at desks, staring blankly at monitors with their heads in their hands. The stragglers are slowly packing up torn tents under the weight of a two-day hangover. By midday, the last of the revellers have left and I find myself alone among the poplar trees, watching the litter-pickers go to work like carrion crows on a battlefield.

It was not meant to be like this. I had picked up a leaflet for Helenesee the previous day which showed happy people splashing about in the water, eating ice-creams and relaxing on the warm sands. It looked like a fine place to rest and rejuvenate before the final push, but I have arrived on a wet and windy Monday, out of season and out of fun.

I could have pressed on to Berlin but couldn't face battling through big city traffic, so I walked down to the empty beach and shivered for a while in the cold wind. I bought a coffee from a little store whose shelves were empty save for the previous day's newspapers and loaves of stale bread; the coffee tasted like despair – a watery, flavourless puddle in a polystyrene cup that was enough to get me back on my bike and heading toward the nearest town.

Frankfurt an der Oder is an odd place: a curious mix of beautiful medieval churches, drab communist, concrete, and cheap plastic modernity. I spent a couple of hours wandering round, trying to convince myself this was interesting, but it was a losing battle. I returned to the campsite with the intention of packing up and finding somewhere more interesting, but by the time I got back the rain had picked up and

Party time.

The other side of the coin – bored, tired, wet and lonely. Killing time in Helenesee.

I decided to accept defeat. Some days are just like that, bummers from the get-go; if I'd learnt anything over the past few weeks, it was to accept the inevitable and to try and make the best of it. So I set to work on productive tasks that could be achieved despite the rain, checking the bike over, tidying and rearranging my belongings, writing notes and rating the various beers I'd collected from the supermarket.

By early evening, the rain had become a downpour. I sat in my little tent, half drunk, bored and lonely, watching beads of water chase each other down the transparent covering of the entrance. The wheel had turned once more, and this time it had come to rest in a quagmire.

To pass the time, I flicked through photos, re-read notes, tried to remind myself what an extraordinary time I'd had, but as the rain fell I couldn't help wondering again what the hell I was doing out here. Was there a point to this? A reason why I had risked life and limb on those crazy Russian motorways and slippery Norwegian passes? If there was, I couldn't see it in the mud and ghostly silhouettes of this empty forest, where I sat alone, peering out at endless trees slowly fading into an eerie gloom as night began to fall.

Then, to my surprise, a young couple came ambling out of the darkness, a little dog straining on its lead in front of them and a small child sat on his father's shoulders, gazing out at the wet world beyond. I'd have forgiven them for hurrying past me because I must have looked a weird type, sat alone in my tent, in the middle of an empty forest, chugging on an oversized bottle with only a motorbike for company. But that didn't stop these nice people from shouting hello, and then, when I returned their greeting, walking over to chat briefly.

The child was transfixed by the Kawasaki and his father placed him on the seat, where he stared at the clocks and the switches with a look of comical delight. I fussed the dog a little and we spoke in broken dialect about this place and the previous days' festivities. Before they went on their way, they told me with all the optimism they could muster that the weather would probably be better tomorrow and that I should look forward to a lovely ride home. It seemed a pitiful lie, but I was grateful nonetheless, and later, as I zipped up my sleeping bag and put down my book, I wondered whether some answers were not to be found amid this lonely old forest after all.

Salvation

The next day was sunny and warm, somewhere. But not any place near me. The rain continued to fall heavily as I rode along the E30 past Berlin, toward Hanover. The conditions were very treacherous, largely on account of the great plumes of spray hurled up by the traffic. But the lack of visibility didn't slow the cars, whose drivers were clearly blessed with some kind of supernatural insight. They continued to fly past me at great speed, far too quickly to slow by any relevant margin should the need arise. I was not happy travelling at such pace so I moved into the slow lane and tucked in behind a convoy of big trucks, finding safety in the shadow of the beast.

At the services, I escaped disaster by the narrowest of margins. With the nozzle of the petrol pump held deep inside the fuel tank I repeatedly squeezed the lever, but for some reason the fuel wouldn't flow. Eventually I gave up and angrily asked the attendant why the machine wouldn't work. She explained that the person who last used the pump had yet to pay, adding as an afterthought: "You do know that's diesel?"

A matter of seconds; that is all that separated me from catastrophe. If the queue at the till had been two people less,

Morning in the Helenesee forest.

the chap in front of me would have made his purchase and I'd have brimmed my tank with that engine-wrecking concoction. As soon as I'd turned the key, the diesel would have flowed down the fuel lines into the carburettors, fouling the plugs, seeping into every nook and cranny like a contaminated blood transfusion.

I had to sit down. Calm down. I was rushing now and mistakes were creeping in. If I wasn't careful, they would start occurring on that sodden motorway too, when I wouldn't have the luxury of a few seconds grace. I forced myself to stop for 30 minutes, to breathe, eat, drink, relax. I was calmer when I got back on the bike and the next few miles were easier, but I was still glad when I pulled off the motorway and eventually found comfort in a charming little guesthouse in the quiet village of Mittevonnirgends.

The owners of the Gästehaus Kim were about as German as you could find outside of a very lazy parody. If they'd been English they would have dressed in tweed, carried a walking cane and held a Labrador on a leash. But for all the comedy stereotypes, their home was lovely and their hospitality delightful. I draped my saturated belongings over warm radiators and tried not to make too much of a mess.

As I rifled through my belongings, sorting the hopelessly drenched from the uncomfortably damp, I couldn't help but think about what a horrible day it had been. How sad to spend the final hours of this extraordinary adventure dawdling along featureless motorways in the rain. But this was always likely to be the case; ever since I sketched out that ludicrously optimistic map months ago, I knew it was going to be tough to do it all. Yet unbelievably I'd managed to hit almost every key objective along the way, and unearth some wonderful surprises, too.

It had been hard work, but what of true value isn't? I reached into my tank bag and removed the letter from Amy, which she'd placed surreptitiously among my belongings with clear instructions not to be opened until my first night on the road. It had been my companion on this trip; lifting my spirits during bad times and reminding me to come home when the going was too good to think about stopping. And almost lost among the kind words of support was a little sentence which I realised, upon re-reading it, perfectly captured the spirit of this journey.

"Have fun, be surprised, get annoyed, get frustrated, get lost and find someplace unexpected because you got lost!"

If I'd been searching for a reason for this adventure then I need not have looked beyond those words. I'd been trying to justify everything in terms of enjoyment or excitement, and when I had struggled to feel happy or thrilled I began to worry that I was somehow failing to make the most of the trip. But in reality, the highs and lows, the ups and downs, the constant revolutions of that sturdy old wheel were the trip. It was not about a delirious ride through sunny meadows filled with bouncing lambs and pretty daisies; the experience was the reason I was doing this; good or bad made no difference, in the end it all came together to define a single, extraordinary whole.

The answer that I'd been seeking had been with me all along, tucked away in an envelope underneath a pile of disorganised currency, maps and documents. But it had taken the best part of 6000 miles for its meaning to become clear. In that little German guesthouse it dawned on me that it was never about enjoying the trip; it was about experiencing it. Without getting annoyed, frustrated and lost I could never really be happy, calm or, erm, found.

Now I clearly understood what I was doing out here on the road and also why I had finally had enough. I had done what

A nice surprise near the German border – I only came in for a sandwich.

I didn't really think I could; it had been a thousand times harder than I expected, but the graft was almost over and the challenge all but complete. Soon the peripheral boredom of the long motorway miles and the misery of rain-soaked days would fall away, leaving a core of beautiful memories that I would cherish for the rest of my life.

At the time it felt like a revelation, but in hindsight it sounds like a cliché. No matter, I did not set off in search of originality. I will take my little cliché and pack it up along with the rest of my belongings in my bulging panniers and straining tank bag and I will ride the final few hundred miles of this adventure a happy and contented man. Well, most of it, anyway.

9
Full circle

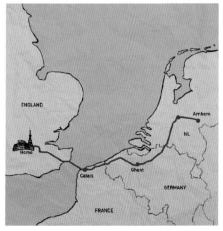

Time for reflection in the Netherlands.

If you ever find yourself in Arnhem and are trying to get anywhere other than the zoo or Utrecht you have my sympathy. I had intended to pass quickly through the city, heading south toward Eindhoven and then across toward Belgium, but the Dutch were very concerned that I shouldn't leave their country without seeing either their fourth largest city or some monkeys. So I made my way west, then at the last minute veered south, detouring below Utrecht and making a break for freedom via the hopelessly congested Antwerp ring road.

It was late afternoon when I pulled up to the Blaarmeersen campsite in the pretty little city of Ghent, just before the French/Belgian border. I'd made a little time over the previous few days and so I allowed myself the sentimental indulgence of ending the journey where it had begun.

I stopped outside the reception office. Three weeks had passed since I'd last stood there; three weeks of hardship, revelation, exultation and all-round madness, and now it was over. Job done, mission complete. I sighed; I had expected to be overcome by a wave of emotion, but instead I just felt empty. I filled out the forms, made polite conversation, then rode round to my allocated spot and put up my tent one last time.

Next to me, a group of English lads struggled to do the same. They argued and laughed and swore at each other amid

Back where it all began: last night at the Blaarmeersen campsite, Ghent.

poles and pegs and canvas and I watched with amusement as they failed repeatedly and with good nature. We chatted briefly and they explained excitedly how they had driven their mum's hatchback down from the north of England, across the channel, and then along 80 miles of manic Continental motorway to this large and friendly campsite, where their adventure had now culminated. They asked where I was heading and I told them back home, to London.

"Not far then," said the older lad, with a hint of condescension in his voice.

I smiled.

"Far enough," I replied.

They didn't ask where I'd come from and I wasn't too concerned about telling them.

Later that evening I made a sort of pilgrimage to the plot where I had stayed on the first night; it seemed right, if not exactly necessary. There was a big camper van parked where my little tent had stood, and outside it sat an elderly couple, reading their newspapers as the warm evening sun set slowly behind them.

I'd hoped to find some poignancy in returning to this place, where I'd bedded down on that first night, with wet gloves and an anxious heart, but in reality it was just another patch of grass. As much as I wanted to, I couldn't get nostalgic over it. I nodded to the old fellow who'd glanced up from his newspaper and was staring at me over his glasses in a determined manner. He didn't respond, just kept staring, so I turned on my heel and was all but gone when the woman shouted after me: "You English?" She had a Scottish accent and I prepared to

The hero of the story: Kawasaki Ninja A1P – the perfect sports tourer.

run, but then the man answered her: "Aye, he is. I heard him talkin' in the wee shop earlier, didn't I son?"

"Maybe," I replied, cautiously, wracking my brains for anything I'd said that might have caused offence.

"Well, come and sit yourself down, lad," said the woman with a smile. "You'll be wanting a beer, will you?"

Before I knew what was happening I found myself seated with two of the friendliest people I have ever met, drinking Belgian beer (and, later, Scotch whisky), and chatting long into the night about travel and adventure, and the many, oft ill-paved roads that constitute life's journey.

I couldn't have wished for a better conclusion to this extraordinary adventure. The universe is full of mad probabilities that seem to hint at design over chance. As humans, we are preconditioned to seek meaning in coincidence, and, under the multitude of stars shining out across that clear Belgian sky, I found myself aching to believe some fortuitous path had led me directly to this encounter. It seemed so unlikely that simple chance could have resulted in my stumbling across these friendly, welcoming, English-speaking people on the exact spot where my journey had begun, providing the perfect bookend to the adventure. And if I weighed up all the good fortune I'd experienced these last three weeks, I couldn't ignore the sense that some benevolent force was at work.

How many times had I turned left and, in so doing, avoided catastrophe down the right-hand path? How often had I stopped to ask for assistance and ended up meeting *the* most helpful person possible under the circumstances? In the whole of St Petersburg I couldn't have chanced across anyone more helpful than Alex; I could say the same for those two kindly gents in Daugavpils, and many others along the way.

With the right kind of eyes it would be so easy to see the hand of God at work. And if not God, then mom, always there to save me from my own stupidity with a reassuring whisper; guiding, nudging, gently influencing my journey toward a safe and happy conclusion. But it is very easy on a drunken night in the company of pleasant strangers to allow fate and superstition free reign over one's emotions. The truth is, coincidence is just that, and there is no place in my world for fairies; the garden is beautiful enough.

'Science,' I reminded myself 'is the search for the ultimate question; religion, the quest for an easy answer.'

It had been a strange evening. Strange in an overpowering, wonderful kind of way, but strange, nonetheless. As the conversation finally wound down and long yawns interrupted the flow, it seemed the time had come to say goodnight. I felt like I'd made two lifetime friends, but in truth I knew I'd never see these people again; in a queer sort of way, that seemed like a fitting epitaph to the whole journey.

An end

Poland seemed a long way away as I waited for the Eurotunnel train to whisk me out of France and back to England. I sat astride the Kawasaki, waiting for the line of cars ahead to slowly move through passport control, flicking through the photos on my phone, and trying to determine the chronology and context of the last three weeks.

Norway was a very distant memory, hardly related to the mad dash back through Europe or the weirdness and danger of Moscow. But Russia, too, felt strangely detached, like a bad jolt of turbulence on an otherwise gentle flight. I struggled to square my time there with the rest of the adventure, perhaps because it had been such a unique experience in itself. It had happened, I was

Almost home and letting the train do the hard work.

"Welcome home; now go and shave!" Amy wonders what's lurking in the undergrowth!

sure of that. I had ridden my motorbike into the heart of that dark empire and lived to tell the tale. But, with hindsight, it felt more like something I'd observed than been a willing party to; perhaps the wounds were still too raw to dwell upon.

It had been a serious ride; a genuine test of mind and soul. Only a fool would have ridden a sports bike into the maelstrom, but maybe it required a certain type of fool to find his way back out. Anyone with sense would have given up long ago.

There was no doubt it had been too much; I had raced when I should have ambled and I had ambled when I should have slept. I'd squeezed a two month trip into three weeks, and turned what might have been a lovely vacation into a painful struggle against time and reason.

But it had been my choice, and there are a lot of people in this world who face greater hardships every hour than I experienced during that journey. People who do not have the luxury of insurance and breakdown cover, and people who would have traded places with me in an instant at any point along the way.

If I had won – and I wasn't sure I had – then it had been a pyrrhic victory, full of sacrifice, hardship, and folly. But it is those same difficulties which lend a motorcycle adventure that critical edge, differentiating it from a vacation. Most holidaymakers do not end up alone and weeping by the roadside as the light starts to fade and the wolves begin to howl. Similarly, the prospect of being crushed repeatedly by a convoy of thundering trucks rarely features in holiday brochures.

But it is in these situations that you find the dirt, and it is in the dirt that you will find the essence of a country, not in the smiling faces of the tourist board reps. I had tasted the dirt of Europe, Russia, and Scandinavia, too, and while the initial hit was troubling, it had a pleasing aftertaste.

Now the ride was almost over and with it the adventure. Somewhere in the distance, Crystal Palace beckoned. I turned the key in the ignition, prodded the starter and felt the Kawasaki spin into life beneath me. It was a fine sensation, as comforting as a glass of good port on a cold winter's eve.

That familiar, reassuring engine note burbled from the exhaust, rising slightly as I eased out the clutch and opened the throttle. It was time to go home. 'Why not?' I thought, 'that Pole was full of good ideas ...'

The End

Appendix – A hapless guide to travelling light

What you take on a trip depends on so many factors it almost seems pointless listing them. Most people like to be prepared, but preparation is subjective; one person's imperatives are another's luxuries; and really, how many pairs of pants do you need?

In my experience, if you don't know what you require then you're probably not ready to head off. By that, I mean that in planning your trip you will inevitably come to a point when you think, 'fuck it, what I don't have I'll either do without or pick up along the way.' That's about the time when you're good to go. On this journey, I rode 6000 miles in three weeks on an ageing sports bike; everything I had was bundled into a rucksack, a tankbag and two panniers. I never felt I hadn't enough space, and if I'd had more, I wouldn't have known what to do with it.

Here's what I took:

Luggage

I wasn't entirely convinced by my Oxford Sports panniers when I first bought them; too difficult to attach, and a bit unwieldy. That was 2006 and I'm still using them. They're tough, spacious and, providing you get the covers on in time, surprisingly waterproof. Lots of pockets, well-made and versatile; still a bugger to attach in the rain though!

A fully loaded tankbag is a must for resting your chin on at traffic lights. It's also the perfect place to keep valuables and important documents because it's easy to take off and carry around when away from the bike. The waterproof cover on my Oxford tankbag makes it a perfect place to store phones, etc, in a downpour; just remember, the cover goes on the outside, right, Rich ...

Tent

I know people spend hundreds of pounds on tents, but I don't really see the point unless you're anticipating truly horrendous conditions. My tent sits nicely on the back of the bike, is spacious enough to house everything I need, and goes up and down in about five minutes. Best of all, it only cost GBP40.

Clothing

Something else that it's so easy to spend a fortune on for no good reason. I've never found anything that'll keep you properly dry in a monster storm, so I just use some cheap over-trousers to keep my legs and boots dry-ish, and then get wet everywhere else. It's not ideal but chances are you'll ride out of the rain at some point and soon dry off in the wind. Again, there's so much kit out there designed to be touring-friendly, but to my mind, you're best sticking with your tried-and-trusted gear that is already broken-in and comfortable. That applies to

Everything you need for three weeks on the road.

jacket, trousers, boots, gloves, lid and back protector. Don't forget ear plugs, and leave the tinted visor at home.

Extras

Puncture repair and tool kit: didn't need either but wouldn't want to be without them. Both fit snugly under the pillion seat.

Motorcycle phone charger: I purchased this off Amazon as a spur of the moment thing just before I left. It was about GBP25 and I was sure it wouldn't work, or if it did, wouldn't last. I was wrong on both counts, and it proved itself extremely useful. No more leaving phones and cameras unattended in camp sites and cafés while they charge. I was a bit concerned it might drain my battery but it didn't seem to have any adverse effects. A brilliant bit of kit: www.amazon. co.uk/Motorcycle-Motorbike-Scooter-hard-wired-Universal/dp/B00AMDI34U/ ref=cm_cr_pr_product_top

The bike

There are plenty of bikes better suited to a trip like this, but I don't own them, so I took my Ninja and it coped admirably. This is a largely stock bike: no touring add-ons (except the above-mentioned charger); original suspension, engine and gearing. It just goes to show how well built modern motorbikes are. I put it in for a service when I got back and the only issue was a leaky rocker cover. Astonishing reliability, reasonable comfort, speed when you need it, and the ability to creep along over small boulders, too!

Michelin Pilot Road 3

It was somewhere in Poland – well into the trip – when I met a British couple out for a spin on their Triumph Tiger. I said where I'd come from, and the chap, Paul, asked when I'd replaced the tyres. He refused to believe they were the same ones I'd left home on. I

couldn't blame him; I was absolutely amazed at the performance and longevity of these boots especially given what they had to contend with in Russia and Latvia. Brilliant grip in the wet or dry and a few thousand miles of rubber left on them at the end of it all. An exceptional tyre and I'm not being paid to say that (but I'd like to be!).

Other important stuff

Currency: Norway is very expensive, but it evens out when you get to Eastern Europe. I budgeted for about GBP60 a day – kept across various wallets and stored in various places – and I came home with some spare cash (but not much). I found it useful to keep a piece of paper to hand with a basic exchange rate for each currency, so I could quickly determine roughly how much I was spending.

Documents

The usual, plus the getting-into-Russia stuff. Take everything to do with your bike, and make sure your insurance and recovery includes Russia. See page 72 but to recap: Visa, passport, driving licence, travel insurance, entry voucher, international driving permit, MoT, bike insurance, vehicle tax and V5 document (and the mythical third-party insurance I never had).

Vaccinations

Not cheap (about GBP300) and hopefully unnecessary, but recommended nonetheless. I received stabbings for:

Tetanus/Diphtheria/Polio
Tick-borne Encephalitis
Typhoid
Hepatitis A & B (not entirely necessary, but when the nurse heard I was travelling by motorbike she suggested it in case I fell off and required a blood transfusion. Quite worrying on just about every level).

Fuel

I was surprised and relieved to discover that petrol of decent quality was never hard to come by in any of the countries I travelled through. But still, a translation sheet was one of my smarter moves. This might help (but please double-check for yourself, and don't treat it as gospel, I have been known to get things quite wrong ...):

Unleaded petrol in:

Belgium, Germany: Super Plus

France: Sans plomb

The Netherlands: Ongelood, or Euro 95, Super 98

Denmark, Sweden, Norway: Blyfri

Finland: Lyijytön bensiini

Russia: НЕЭТИЛИРОВАННЫЙ БЕНЗИН – or anything with an A and a backward N, (АИ). I think I also saw it referred to as devyanosto pyaty)

Latvia: Bezsvina

Lithuania: Bešvinis benzinas

Poland: Benzyna bezołowiowa (PB – Eurosuper or Superplus)

Many thanks to Sam and Amy for the maps; Sam for the brilliant illustrations; Paul, Mike and Amy for the proofreading, and for knowing what I meant when I couldn't work out how to say it properly; John and Julie for rebuilding our house while I was away(!); all at Veloce for their support and assistance; Bob for the stylish poncho; and everyone who helped me throughout the journey – much appreciated!

Latest motorcycle titles from Veloce

Bonjour! Is this Italy?

Following his dismissal from a job he never should have had, the author packs a tent, some snacks, and a suit, and sets out on a two-wheeled adventure across Europe. Includes maps and illustrations, hints and tips, places to stay, plus valuable first-hand guidance on what to do when things go wrong.

ISBN: 978-1-845843-99-1
Paperback • £12.99* UK/$$24.95* USA • 144 pages

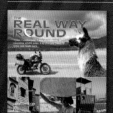

The Real Way Round

A pictorial diary of a once-in-a-lifetime motorbike trip across 35 countries, and a practical guide to motorcycling round the world – what to do first, what to plan for, and how to cope with the unexpected.

ISBN: 978-1-845842-94-9
Hardback • £40* UK/$59.95* USA • 224 pages

TT Talking

From a race in decline, to the World's most famous and iconic road race, TT Talking tells the story of one of the most dramatic eras in the history of the Isle of Man Tourist Trophy. Charlie Lambert tells the story of this sensational upturn, from his own role behind the microphone, to the pressures, controversies, laughs, and sadness that go with being the man at the heart of the world's most famous road race.

ISBN: 978-1-845847-50-0
Paperback • £14.99* UK/$24.95* USA • 160 pages

For more info on Veloce titles, visit our website at www.veloce.co.uk email: info@veloce.co.uk Tel: +44(0)1305 260068
* prices subject to change, p&p extra